BACK OF THE BOAT
GOURMET COOKING

Borgo Press Books by William Maltese:

THE TRAVELING GOURMAND SERIES:

Back of the Boat Gourmet Cooking: Afloat—Pool-Side—Backyard (with Bonnie Clark) (#2)
The Gluten-Free Way: My Way (with Adrienne Z. Milligan) (#1)
William Maltese's Wine Taster's Guide: Spokane/Pullman Washington Wine Region (#3)

BACK OF THE BOAT GOURMET COOKING

AFLOAT—POOL-SIDE—BACKYARD

The Traveling Gourmand, Book Two

by

BONNIE CLARK

& WILLIAM MALTESE

THE BORGO PRESS

An Imprint of Wildside Press LLC

MMX

Copyright © 2010 by Bonnie Clark & William Maltese
Cover Graphic by Deana C. Jamroz

All rights reserved.
No part of this book may be reproduced in any form
without the expressed written consent
of the authors and publisher.
Printed in the United States of America

www.wildsidebooks.com

FIRST EDITION

CONTENTS

Dedications 7
Disclaimer.. 8
Prologues 9
Gas or Charcoal and Other Things 16
Additional Equipment Needs 20
Basic Equipment List 21

RECIPES

Starters and Snacks... 29
Eggs 39
Vegetables 41
Salads.. 51
Fish and Seafood 63
Meat.. 77
Poultry (Chicken) 97
Pasta.. 105
Bread... 111
Pizza 123
Dips/Salsas/Sauces/Spreads 133

Butters/Dressings/Oils/Vinaigrettes 151
Desserts 163
Drink 173
URLs 176

Recipe Index 179
About the Authors 185

DEDICATIONS

BONNIE—

To my husband, *Bruce*, the love of my life and the center of my world, who has always given me the support and encouragement to follow my dreams and who happily fired up the grill and ate all those experiments.

To my Mother, *May*, who taught me the love of cooking and entertaining.

And, of course, to *William Maltese*, who inspired me to write this book. Without William, I would still be wishing *someone* would write a book like this.

WILLIAM—

To *Bonnie* and *Bruce* for the text. To *Laura* and *Deana* for the cover. To *John*, and *Michael*, and *Wildside/Borgo* for the publication. To the readers for the reading.

DISCLAIMER

All organizations, businesses, and product names mentioned in this book are the property of those individual organizations and businesses. In this day and age of the internet when so many organizations, businesses, and products are so often made mention of without their attending trademark designates ™ or ®, it's difficult to know when or if to provide these indicators. Even specific searches of U.S. Trademark Department files can often be confusing. So, more often than not, the authors have erred on the side of inclusion, rather than exclusion. If mistakes have been made, we shall make every attempt to make sure they're corrected in any subsequent editions of this book.

PROLOGUES

BONNIE—

My husband, Bruce, and I have been boating people seemingly since Day One. Actually, Bruce started long before I did; his family had a summer house on Diamond Lake in Washington State. Bruce grew up on the water, and I grew to love it, too; although, I never did get up on skis or learn to swim very well. Being a redhead, I was, and still am, best at sun-burning.

Bruce and I bought our first boat soon after we married. At that time, the extent of our boating eats consisted of cold sandwiches and chips. The sandwiches were mostly peanut butter and jam as those didn't need to be kept cool. The boat was too small to have a very big ice chest, and we needed the room in the cooler for drinks—usually colas as we were not old enough to buy liquor, having been married quite young. We would pull into a deserted cove—usually one with a "No Trespassing" sign nailed to a tree on the shoreline, spread out our blanket on the beach, make our sandwiches, eat them, and, then, be back on the water in no time (hopefully before being kicked off). Oh, those were the days!

When our children came along, we needed a bigger boat, as well as one we could use for skiing; Bruce and our kids, our friends and their kids, loved to ski; mainly, I babysat on the shore.

About that time, too, those little hibachis and cheap little BBQ's became popular; perfect to take to the lake to use at the launch areas, or on the beaches. With one of those, we were able to graduate from peanut-butter-and-jam sandwiches to burgers and hot dogs. With that change, we thought we had really moved up the food chain!

Then, Bruce took a job that required him to be on-call evenings and weekends; that put our boating on-hold. Eventually, albeit reluctantly, we sold our boat; we installed a swimming pool at our house, instead. Our family, friends, and our children's friends, came to our house instead of to the lake. At that time, I really got into barbecuing, if just because I didn't want to be in the house, cooking, while everyone else was out at the pool having fun. Besides, being the worry-wart that I was, I had to be at poolside to kept track of everyone and make sure they were obeying all the rules; I had lots of rules!

Poolside, I would put whatever we were eating on "cruise control"; meaning, I mainly used the BBQ rotisserie, because it didn't need much watching. To make everything even easier, I bought each and every rotisserie gadget and basket I could find.

I learned to plan ahead to make dinners simpler, faster, and easier. I learned a lot of shortcuts, right there at the house, which, later on, proved invaluable for our return to boating and our final upgrade to some truly Back of the Boat Gourmet Cooking.

Therefore, you'll find the recipes in this book not only provide you with fine dining on your boat, but, if you so desire, at pool-side, in your backyard, or while picnicking, camping, or fishing.

NOTE: No matter how much planning and preparing is done ahead of time, whoever does the grilling will invariably get all the applause for the fabulous food; in our case that *someone* is usually Bruce who just always smiles and says, "Thank you!" The bugger!

As I've already hinted, my husband and I, once the children were grown and out of the house, spent less time around the pool and, again, started thinking of our return to boating. By then, we'd pretty much excluded skiing from our recreational repertoire, and we were more interested in somewhere close to spend some getaway leisurely time—whether with friends, or just by our lonesome—and eat.

There are a lot of lakes in our area, but Coeur d'Alene Lake, in northern Idaho, is the closest large one that allows us docking facilities for convenient midweek access for sunset dinners, cruising, or just lazily summer drifting while eating plump and juicy Washington State strawberries dipped in chocolate fondue made with Xoçai® (The Healthy Chocolate), and/or while relaxing with a chilled glass of Washington State Latah Creek Muscat Cannelli. That's where you'll most likely find us, too, every weekend and evenings during the April to October Pacific Northwest boating season.

WILLIAM—

As someone who was born and raised in the Pacific Northwest, a locale known for its preponderance of lakes and rivers...someone who's from an extended family that took its fishing damned seriously...and someone who has had the great pleasure, over the years, of having been on board ocean-going yachts and ships that boast extensive galleys and, even, extensive kitchen staffs...I've had a very long and very enjoyable exposure to the pleasures inherent in boating and the food available on board.

Early on in my life, fine dining on the water wasn't of first consideration—if, in fact, of any consideration at all—in that food consumption consisted mainly of chowing-down on whatever was conveniently packed (in paper-bag, lunchbox, or cooler) for an excursion. While this could mean any number of selections from the available menu of cold-cuts, cold fried chicken, cheese, potato salad, milk, even an apple, the closest any of this ever genuinely came to gourmet dining was on our return to the evening's campfire, or to the convenient cabin's kitchen, where the fresh catch of the day was converted into mouth-watering fried or grilled fish for much-enjoyed end-of-day feasting.

My university days saw me chumming with a crowd of young recreational boaters that could boast several watercraft, none larger than thirty feet, all with skippers and "crews" who had discovered pre-packaged meals were no longer nearly as "in" and/or as fashionable as the newly discovered wonders of freshly barbecued hot dogs and hamburgers, supplemented by crisp chips and ice-cold beer, all of which fit to a tee all of our college-boys' admittedly indiscernible palates.

Eventually, when I became more "a man of the world," I graduated to cruises on the high seas aboard immense ocean liners whose humongous galleys were able to set before me a whole array of genuinely delicious foods stuff that could, and did, rival anything served up by the best restaurants in the world.

Then, of course, there were my leisurely spent halcyon days on several yachts whose owners had their captains and crews ply the waters of the Mediterranean, Caribbean, and South Seas, and daily harvest fresh seafood from the surrounding waters, to be set upon by a cook, and sometimes attending staff, in galleys that, while they didn't rival those of any cruise-line steamship, still provided some truly memorable eating experiences.

As a result, I early came to believe that the caliber of my dining on water depended entirely upon the size of the craft in which I "sailed." A rowboat would likely still see me brown-bagging it; something smaller than thirty-feet would likely see me dining on weenies and hamburgers; larger than thirty-feet would likely see me enjoying the benefits of a fully-equipped galley and someone likely "on staff" capable of preparing some really fine meals; luxury liners, while no longer as capable of providing fine dining as they once did, still remained the closest to a restaurant experience.

This misconception, of course, changed, but only when I was able to reunite, after a long absence, with my cousin, Bonnie, and with her husband Bruce, who, with their long history as boat owners, had somehow managed, on their thirty-foot boat, to jettison the old stereotype of nothing available on-board but hot dogs and hamburgers. Dining aboard the Clark's boat, in fact, includes a whole repertoire of fine-dining gourmet cooking that can not only be as easily managed and advantaged on a rowboat but on the deck of the grandest yacht if and when a viable option is wanted that doesn't necessitate dirtying every pot and pan in a ship's extensive galley.

The proof of my cousin and her husband's success in the onboard cooking miracles they've achieved is no better illustrated than by the number of times I have seen boats of all sizes, on Lake Coeur d'Alene, gravitate from all around, like iron filings to a magnet, to have the people on board hail the Clarks and inquire as to what "smells so damned delicious," often times sticking around long enough to be provided with samples and, in return, provide rave reviews.

As a direct result of my having seen, first hand, what is achievable by my cousin, by way of gourmet dining, on a small craft, or on large, with a minimum amount of equipment, time, and effort, I have been on an joint quest with the Clarks to find even more new and exciting recipes to add to those already devised by Bonnie and her husband. It being our sole purpose, and, now, that of our publisher, Wildside/Borgo Press, to clue in small boat owners to the still little-known fact that they needn't eat only hot dogs and hamburgers, and to let the larger boat owners know that it's not always necessary for fine dining to go any farther than a small propane grill affixed to their yacht's outside railing.

And, of course, for those of you who don't own a boat, large or small, probably never will, or don't really ever want to, there's nothing here that you can't whip up just as easily on solid ground, whether or not at a backyard barbecue, or on a picnic, or just while camping out.

Wherever, whenever...smooth sailing...and *bon appétit!*

GAS OR CHARCOAL AND OTHER THINGS

BONNIE—

Never, ever, use a charcoal grill on a boat, not even if you're a BBQ purist who thinks food can't get that wonderfully smoky flavor from a gas grill. Charcoal fires and boats just don't go together. What's more, charcoal grills aren't made to be attached to a boat, so the risk of the grill tipping, when a wave hits, spilling hot coals, can be dangerous in the extreme; plus, what to do with those hot coals and/or ashes after you're done grilling? Dumping them in the lake is not an environmentally friendly option, no matter how tempting. In fact, don't dump *anything* in *any* lake.

Some of our fellow boat owners have full-size charcoal grills on the docks by their boats. While such grills are nice to have, they do require that you come back into the marina to use them, and that can be frustrating if you have to interrupt the fun you're having out on the water. Besides which, such grills have a decided tendency to be top heavy and don't maintain their balance very well on rocking docks, especially in bad weather—and docks DO rock—and the wind DOES blow—and more than one fish has ended up with a meal intended for boaters.

Marine stores carry a line of propane grills that are specifically made for the back or side of a boat. Use one of those, in that they are designed to attach with brackets to the rail, or even to a fishing-pole holder. Be sure yours is one with a lid, and that the lid is attached. The first grill we purchased had a lid that wasn't attached, and we almost lost it overboard the first time we used it. Bruce was quick and caught it just before it disappeared into the lake. His playing Hot Potato with the hot lid was a little too exciting, though, especially with guests on board. After that, he attached the lid to its grill with a chain. In fact, I can't even imagine why manufacturers make their products with unattached lids. Bruce put a safety chain on our whole grill, as well; since then, we've still seen several of our fellow boaters' grills go overboard.

Certainly, we recommend that when buying your grill, you, also, get the overall "storage" cover they sell for the grills. They're a bit pricey, but pay for themselves by saving your boat from grease stains and protecting your grill whenever you're not using it.

Grills come in different sizes. Get the size that fits your purpose; although, Bruce and I, now on our third grill, have upgraded to a larger one each time. Some of these grills even have legs so they can be transferred to the dock or beach. We keep one of our old grills in our dock box to use for large dock parties, or when we tie up with other boaters for progressive dinners that require an extra grill or two.

Also, from the get-go, pay attention to your particular grill's idiosyncrasies, in that not all grills are created equal. Some burn hotter than others. For instance, take the one bought by Craig, one of our dock neighbors. Although it's the very same brand of grill as bought by my husband, from the very same store, on the very same day, and of the very same size (heaven forbid one guy should have "anything" bigger than the other), Craig's grill cooks at a much higher temperature. As a result, he and we are always having "friendly" Battles of the Grills. "Hey, Bruce and Bonnie, are you planning to eat sometime tonight?" "Hey, Craig, why do you always burn food on the outside and leave it so raw on the inside?" Admittedly, these grills each come with a knob that turns its flame up or down, but it may take you some time to master the "how" of getting the flame that works just right for you.

Workspace, on a boat, next to the grill, is really important; plan to have lots of it. The usual juggling of food, plates, pots, pans, and utensils, is even harder while riding the waves in front of a hot grill. Some of the marine grills have "mate tables" that attach to their fronts, but, on some boats, there just isn't enough room to have these inserted between you and a cooking surface. So, it's better that you get the kind of table that attaches to the boat railing *next to* the grill. Some of these even fold down, out of the way, when not in use.

The best thing I've discovered about these grills is that they can double as gas stoves. Sporting goods and discount stores, such as Target, carry pans for specific use on camp-stoves with convenient fold-down handles that work well for the grill and for storing. The best is cast-iron skillets. They are heavy and work well on a gas grill, and they don't have to be washed. Just wipe them out with a paper towel or a damp rag. Be sure, though, that they're thoroughly dry before putting them away or they'll rust.

TIP: Always be sure you have plenty of extra propane. Sometimes, we end up with a couple extra cans onboard, because once, and only once, we ran out of gas (quite literally) before the food was done. If it's any consolation, though, I promise you will only forget once!

ADDITIONAL EQUIPMENT NEEDS

BONNIE—

Our boat has a galley; however, the only thing I've ever made in it is coffee. I don't even know if its stove works! Mainly, I use it for storing equipment and washing the dishes. If your boat doesn't have a galley, only limited storage, just keep everything in a plastic container that'll fit, somewhere, and, maybe, even double for seating. Toss your dirty dishes in a garbage bag to take home with you. That'll keep the boat's official plastic container clean so you'll only have to restock it with clean plates and utensils for your next outing.

By the way, long-handled BBQ tools are really awkward, not to mention dangerous, on a boat. Wooden handles, however, keep you from burning your hands.

BASIC EQUIPMENT LIST

- *Brush, for basting (an inexpensive paintbrush works just fine)*

- *Container with a good-fitting lid*

You'll need this for storing the oily "rag" you'll use to put oil on your grate.

We usually just use an empty Cool Whip® container. Use tongs to swish the oil rag over the grate. Between uses, you should store this container, and its rag, in the refrigerator to keep the old oil on the rag from getting rancid. If you use a brush to oil your grill, you can get dangerous flare-ups as a direct result of drips; you don't need open fire, of any kind, on shipboard.

- *Cooler, small, just for fish*

No matter how fresh seafood is, it can quickly start to smell fishy to a discerning and sensitive nose. It's especially important to keep any seafood as cold as possible, for cooking as quickly as possible. If we're planning a weekend on our boat, we have any fish/seafood the first night, then warm any of the leftovers for the next day. A favorite doubling-up for us is fresh salmon or shrimp grilled the first night, followed by fish cakes, of the shrimp, or salmon, on a bed of greens, either for lunch or for dinner the next day.

- *Corkscrews (two, in that one is always breaking), and a wine-seal cutter*

- *Cutting boards (two)—one for chicken and meat, one for everything else*

- *Dishes and drink containers (acrylic)*

No glass, because of all the bare feet. No stemware, in that it has a tendency to "jump" overboard; we lost countless good wine glasses before we ever figured that out.

Acrylic dishes, acrylic drink containers, flatware, even pans, can easily be washed, on the spot, in only a matter of minutes, or be taken home to be cleaned.

- *Drawer liners, rubber-mesh*

These can be used to keep things from sliding on a rocking boat; everything has a tendency to slide. Just cut them to fit where you need them. We use a wide strip down the center of the table; don't cover the entire table, though, because you'll be putting down hot things, and the mats will melt. We cut smaller pieces to use beneath salt, pepper, condiments, glasses, and whatnot. We use a piece to anchor cutting boards, and it's good for providing that extra bit of grip you need to open the recalcitrant lids of some jars.

- *Griddle and/or flat-plate, cast-iron*
- *Knives, at least chef and paring (good quality)*
- *Pans and baskets (the kind with holes and slots) made specifically for grills*
- *Pans, cast-iron, that fit your grill*
- *Pizza peel or paddle*
- *Pizza slicing wheel*
- *Pot holders and mitts*
- *Rolling pin, small, for rolling out pizza dough*
- *Salad-shooter®*

Not only for salads, but for grating cheese, on and off the boat; it can grate a pound of cheese in nothing flat; which is a lot less expensive, not to mention healthier (less preservatives) than buying cheese pre-shredded in a grocery store.

- *Skewers—metal or wood/bamboo*

Wooden or bamboo skewers need to be soaked in cold water to prevent them from burning.

- *Spatulas, including a wide metal one (for fish, etc.)*

- *Tongs in a variety of shapes and sizes*

- *Utensils (flatware for eight or ten, plus serving pieces and extra tablespoons)*

- *Ziploc® bags in various sizes*

NOTE: While you may think that paper, by way of plates and drinking containers, is the best way to go, that's not always the case when on board a boat. We do use paper, on occasion, but not often, if just because of the major headache of dealing with the resulting garbage problem. With the heat that usually accompanies boating weather, it doesn't take long for food- and/or drink-soiled paper products or disposable utensils to start stinking. Napkins are about the only paper product we use with our meals, although, even there, we prefer cloth, in that cloth won't blow away as easily. We use white 100% cotton napkins which are inexpensive and easy to wash and bleach. Small cloth dish towels work well, too, especially for mopping up any inevitable spill.

We just insert dirty "things" inside Ziploc® plastic bags, zip closed, thereby eliminating nasty smells, and ending up with small and neat packages for any dumpster.

As regards garbage disposal, there admittedly are often garbage cans, or dumpsters, at public docks, or at your marina. Most often, though, you'll find these already overflowing with garbage by the time you're ready to use them; as a conscientious boater, you don't really want or need to contribute to that kind of problem.

Using a grill, you won't usually have a lot of pots and pans needing your clean-up attention.

RECIPES

The following recipes aren't written in stone. The authors are the kinds of cooks who often use a "pinch" of this, a "bunch" of that, and/or a "handful" of whatever. If they don't have the spice or herb they usually use, they invariably use something else that's available. Sometimes the result of such adventuresome experimentation is a better dish than the original. So, you should feel free to experiment, too, taking into account your own particular tastes. The main thing with Back of the Boat Gourmet Cooking, as with any form of cooking, is to enjoy what you're doing and relax while you're doing it. Maybe even have a glass of wine, especially since a splash or two of *vino* has been known to enhance the flavor of more than one dish.

Since boating season invariably coincides with fresh-produce season, stop at your local produce stand, or farmers' market, and plan your menus accordingly. You may find that an original plan to make grilled peach Fruit Crumble changes when it becomes so obvious that plums, apples, nectarines, whatever, are looking so much better than the peaches. The same thing can be said of vegetable selection if something is available that is fresher than your initial choice of the day. In fact, most every ingredient of most any recipe can be either adjusted, or substituted with something else, on the spur of the moment, with sometimes truly amazing flavor combinations that result.

And, since the last thing anyone wants is to stand for a long period, over a hot grill, in the blazing sun, on a boat, in the middle of the lake or in some bay, remember that a lot of that can easily be avoided, shipboard life made simpler and easier, by simply doing as much preplanning as you can before you're on board. While there's not always a lot of time available for pre-preparation, especially with everyone anxious to "hit" the water, a cook's enjoyment of any such weekend may well depend upon utilization of every available short cut.

For example, near the end of the week, on your way home from chores or work, purchase one of those whole roasted chickens from your deli or grocer. Bring it home, pop it into your refrigerator to cool down, and take it to your boat with you. In a pinch, you can pick one up while you're on your way to your boat, but be forewarned that hot chicken will spoil really fast, if you're not careful, and it's sometimes hard to cool it down fast enough, and safely enough, in just an ice chest or cooler. So, any chicken bought in route should be served as soon as possible upon arrival. Leftovers from it should be cut into small pieces, diced, shredded, or thinly sliced, and placed in small containers or Ziploc® bags that can be quickly cooled when stored. Don't over-fill any such containers, either, or, once again, you risk the chicken not cooling safely.

Freshly grated Parmesan cheese can be bought at any deli.

By way of another example, Herb Pasta (See PASTA) can easily be made with pesto from your favorite deli; just thin it down with pasta water when you add the pasta.

If dried herbs are easier, use ½ or less of the amount called for in the recipes, crushing the herbs in your hands to release the oils.

Just don't be afraid to use whatever the shortcut, if and when it makes itself known, because, take it from us, you'll be a happier boater in having done so.

STARTERS AND SNACKS

Jalapeño Poppers

CAUTION: JALAPEÑOS CAN BE VERY HOT. WEAR RUBBER GLOVES IF YOU HAVE SENSITIVE SKIN. KEEP HANDS AWAY FROM YOUR FACE AND EYES AND OTHER SENSITIVE PARTS OF YOUR BODY. WASH HANDS THOROUGHLY WITH SOAP AND WARM WATER WHEN FINISHED HANDLING THE PEPPERS.

12 large jalapeño peppers
¼ pound Jarlsberg cheese, cut to fit the peppers
12 bacon slices
Toothpicks

Preheat grill to high.

Slit each pepper along one side. Carefully open the pepper and remove its seeds and veins. **NOTE:** We've found that a teaspoon works ideally for doing this.

Stuff each pepper with the cheese.

Wrap the bacon slice around each pepper and secure with a toothpick.

Well oil the grate.

Turn grill to medium-high.

Place on preheated grill.

Close the grill lid, but watch your cooking closely, especially if you don't yet "know" your grill.

Cook 3-5 minutes until the bacon is done and the cheese is melted.

Serve hot from the grill.

Remove toothpicks before serving.

RECOMMENDED WINE:

Merry Cellars Gewürztraminer.

NACHOS

As you will be using smaller cast-iron pans on the boat grill, this recipe will make at least two pans. Just divide accordingly.

1 pound bag of corn chips—for a festive look use blue, red and white chips
¾ pound Pepperjack cheese, grated
¾ pound Cheddar Cheese, grated
Sour Cream

Guacamole (See: Dips/Salsas/Sauces/Spreads)
Pico de Gallo (See: Dips/Salsas/Sauces/Spreads)

Preheat your grill to high.

In the bottom of a well-seasoned cast-iron pan, sprinkle a little of the cheese.

Top with ⅓ of the chips and sprinkle with ⅓ of the remaining cheese. Repeat 2 more layers, ending with the cheese.

Turn the grill on low.

With lid down, cook until cheese is melted (about 5 to 7 minutes); if handle of pan sticks out, it's okay.

Remove the pan from grill.

Top with Pico de Gallo, sour cream, and/or Guacamole.

This may, if you prefer, be served as a complete dinner, in and of itself.

NOTE: What we've provided above is merely a basic recipe upon which you should feel free "to build." If you wish to include re-fried beans, cooked ground beef, sausage, hot and/or sweet peppers, by all means do so; just remember that such additions usually always work best if the very first layer down, after the initial sprinkle of cheese, is always chips.

RECOMMENDED WINE:

Santa Ema Merlot
Merry Cellars Sauvignon Blanc
Whitestone Winery Merlot

POTATOES

Idaho, russet, red or white new, fingerlings, etc.

Choose the amount and size that will work best for how you are preparing, remembering the size of your grill, and the amount of time you want to spend over the grill. The bigger the potatoes, the longer the time it'll take to grill them. We like to use small-to-medium potatoes. As an appetizer, though, a small potato is perfect.

At Home:

Cook potatoes in salted water until fork tender. Do not overcook or break the skins.

NOTE: If you intend to make Potatoes with Caviar and Sour Cream (*See Below*), you might prefer to cook the potatoes in unsalted water, in that some people may find the combination of salt imparted to the potato by the water, salt from the bacon, plus the saltiness of the caviar, too salty. Another alternative is to blanch the bacon before using.

Drain and cool potatoes.

Cut cooled potatoes in half, not lengthwise.

Put flat- (cut-) side down on the counter, and, with small end of a melon-baller, scoop *through the skin* to remove some of the potato from the center of each half (leaving the side intact).

Put hollowed-out potato halves, flat- (cut-) side down in a container for transport to the boat.

POTATOES WITH CAVIAR & SOUR CREAM

Potatoes
Bacon
Toothpicks
Sour Cream
Caviar

On boat:

Preheat grill to high.

Well oil the grate.

Wrap each hollowed potato half with bacon, and secure with toothpick.

Put potatoes flat- (cut-) sides down on the grill, and cover loosely with foil.

Turn grill to medium.

Grill 10 to 15 minutes until bacon is done.

Let cool slightly.

Remove toothpicks.

Spoon sour cream into the hollowed-out area of each potato half.

Add a dollop of caviar to the top of the sour cream.

RECOMMENDED WINE:

Mountain Dome sparkling wine
Veuve Clicquot Champagne

POTATOES FOR CHIPS

Potatoes
Butter, melted
Salt and Pepper, freshly ground or Montreal Steak Seasoning
Cheese, of your choice, shredded
Parmesan cheese, if desired (for sprinkling)
Chives, minced
Sour cream

On boat:

Preheat grill to hot.

Well oil the grate.

Slice potatoes ¾" thick, either rounds or lengthwise.

With a pastry brush, apply preferred melted butter to one side (See Butters/Dressings/Oils/Vinaigrettes).

Salt and pepper.

Place potato slices, buttered side down, on grill.

Grill for 4-5 minutes with lid closed.

Butter tops of grilling slices and flip.

Top with the shredded cheese, and sprinkle on Parmesan cheese (if desired).

Cook with lid closed until cheese is melted.

Serve immediately with sour cream, chives, and salt and pepper.

POTATOES FOR STUFFED SKINS

Potatoes
Cheese of your choice, shredded
Chives, minced
Bacon
Toothpicks
Sour cream

On boat:

Preheat grill to high.

Well oil grate.

Into scooped-out areas of the potato halves, stuff shredded cheese and minced chives.

Wrap each stuffed potato half with bacon slice and fasten with a toothpick.

Place bacon-wrapped stuffed potato halves, flat- (cut-) side down on the grill.

Cover loosely with foil.

Close grill lid, but closely watch cooking.

Turn grill down to medium.

Potatoes should be done when the bacon is done and the cheese is melted (approximately 12-17 minutes).

Remove the toothpicks.

Serve with dollops of sour cream.

EGGS

G̲r̲e̲e̲n̲ ̲E̲g̲g̲s̲

Serve with Grilled Ham (See Meat/Ham) for Green Eggs and Ham!

4 eggs
4 tablespoons of water
Salt and pepper, to taste
1 tablespoon Pesto (See Dips/Salsas/Sauces/Spreads)

Preheat the grill.

Break eggs into a bowl.

Add water, Pesto, salt and pepper.

Beat with a fork or whisk until just blended.

Heat a pan on the grill.

Lightly oil the bottom of the pan.

Add egg mixture.

As eggs begin to set, stir gently until set but moist.

Serve immediately.

VEGETABLES

CORN WITH CHILI-LIME BUTTER

4 ears corn, fresh
Chili-Lime Butter (See Butters/Dressings/Oils/Vinaigrettes)

At home:

NOTE: Charred husks can be quite messy on the boat. We prefer to husk them and remove their silk **at home**, then soak de-husked ears in water for about 10 minutes, and, then, wrap each tightly in foil. Or, you carefully peel back the husk from each ear, leave the husk intact but remove all the silk; return the husk to its original wrapping of the ear; then, soak corn and husk in water for about 10 minutes.

Package and refrigerate.

On boat:

Preheat grill to high.

Put the corn (with husks, or with foil) on un-oiled grill; if grilling unwrapped corn, well-oil grill.

NOTE: If grilling with the husks still on, turn until husks are charred on all sides (about 15-20 minutes). If grilling foil-wrapped corn (approx 15 minutes). If grilling unwrapped corn, oil the grate, turn until ears are nicely charred (10-15 minutes).

NOTE: Watch closely, if grilling unwrapped corn, because corn has high sugar content and will burn quickly.

Remove from grill.

Discard any husk or foil.

Serve each ear topped with dollop of Lime-Chili butter.

OTHER VEGETABLES FROM A-Z

Vegetables, from Asparagus to Zucchini, with few exceptions, can be grilled (on or off skewers), on a medium-hot grill. Grill all, or some, for a great "veggie platter," or put them on a pizza, in a pita, or in a wrap, with or without Cream Cheese Dill Spread or Herbed Goat Cheese Spread (See Dips/Salsas/Sauces/Spreads).

Toss prepared vegetables with ¼ cup of olive oil, salt and pepper.

For a simple side-dish—

Grill until *al dente*.

Drizzle with Vinaigrette (See Butters/Dressings/Oils/Vinaigrettes).

ARTICHOKES

At home:

Up to a few hours before grilling, trim the sharp points with scissors.

Squeeze the juice of a half a lemon on the artichokes.

Put the artichokes and remaining partially squeezed lemon half in a large pot with enough cold water to cover.

Add salt (about 2 tablespoons for 4 artichokes).

Put a plate or a small lid on top of the artichokes to hold them under the water.

Boil for about 20 to 25 minutes, until tender.

Cool.

Cut the artichokes in half lengthwise and remove the choke.

Put in an airtight container.

Refrigerate.

On boat:

Preheat grill to hot

Well oil grate.

Grill cut-side down for about 2 minutes, 1 minute on other side.

ASPARAGUS

We like to use large spears, tender not woody.

Trim off the ends and pare the tough skin.

Be sure to put the spears crosswise on the grill so they don't fall through the grate.

NOTE: Asparagus can be skewed for easier handling, or use a grill pan.

Brush asparagus and grate with oil.

Grill 3 to 5 minutes on each side.

Drizzle with the Vinaigrette (See Butters/Dressings/Oils/Vinaigrettes).

Salt and pepper to taste.

EGGPLANTS, ONIONS, ZUCCHINI, AND OTHER SQUASH

Preheat grill to high.

Well oil grate.

Slice ½-inch thick.

Toss with oil or one of the flavored Oils (See Butters/Dressings/Oils/Vinaigrettes).

Grill for about 3 to 4 minutes on each side.

Drizzle with Vinaigrettes (See Butters/Dressings/Oils/Vinaigrettes).

Salt and pepper to taste.

GREEN BEANS

Preheat grill to high.

Well oil grate.

Snap off the stem ends.

Toss with oil or one of the flavored Oils (See Butters/Dressings/Oils/Vinaigrettes)

NOTE: Since green beans easily fall through the grate, use grill pan.

Grill until brown and *al dente*.

Salt and pepper to taste.

PEPPERS (GREEN, YELLOW, RED)

Preheat to high.

Well oil grate.

Grill whole until charred on all sides.

Remove from grill.

Cover for about 20 minutes to steam the skins loose.

NOTE: Placement in a Ziploc® bag works well for this and makes for easy clean-up.

Peel.

NOTE: Do not peel under running water, or you'll lose the char flavor.

Core and seed.

Cut into slices or pieces.

NOTE: They can be put back on grill to reheat, or used for kebabs, or drizzled with Vinaigrette (See Butters/ Dressings/Oils/Vinaigrettes).

MUSHROOMS

Preheat grill to high.

Well oil grate.

NOTE: Portobello mushrooms can be grilled like a steak and served as a main dish, mushroom burger, or as a side dish for a steak.

Do not wash mushrooms, because they're like sponges and soak up water. Brush or wipe dirt off with soft mushroom brush or paper towel.

De-stem for grilling.

Put small mushrooms in bowl and toss with olive oil; for portobello mushrooms, oil separately

Grill gill-side down until golden brown.

Turn and grill until done.

Drizzle with Vinaigrette (See Butters/Dressings/Oils/Vinaigrettes).

Or…

Top with ¼ cup fresh grated Parmesan cheese and 1½ thyme leaves, fresh.

Close the lid on the grill for about 1 minute more until cheese is melted.

Drizzle with olive oil or Garlic Oil (See Butters/Dressings/Oils/Vinaigrettes)

SCALLIONS/GREEN ONIONS

Preheat grill to high.

Well oil grate.

Trim the root ends and the green tops, leaving most of the green.

Lay crosswise on the grill, so they don't fall through the grate.

Grill until done to taste.

TOMATOES

Preheat grill to high.

Well oil grate.

Cut in half.

Grill briefly, cut-side down. Turn and grill briefly. Don't overcook.

Drizzle with Vinaigrette (See Butters/Dressings/Oils/Vinaigrettes)

Salt and pepper to taste.

Or…

Same topping or drizzle as with mushrooms.

SALADS

Salads travel best without mayonnaise. Besides, who wants just another potato or macaroni salad when there are so many wonderful recipes to choose from that are safer for serving up within the heated environment found in summer on board ship?!

Bonnie's Exotic Pasta Salad

NOTE: Any of ingredients that may sound exotic, are usually available in the gourmet section of your local grocery store, or in your favorite gourmet market.

1 pound Multicolored Italian Pasta
9-ounce jar Roasted Garlic and Eggplant Spread
14-ounce can tomatoes, diced, including juice
1 small jar marinated artichoke hearts, diced
3-ounce jar Muffuletta Mix
2 tablespoon fresh basil, chopped
Napastyle® gray salt
Pepper, freshly ground

At Home:

Prepare pasta, according to directions on package to *al denta*.

Drain.

Combine Roasted Garlic and Eggplant Spread with the pasta.

Mix well.

Add the rest of the ingredients, except salt and pepper.

Mix.

Salt and pepper to taste.

Refrigerate.

On boat:

For a quick salad, serve with crusty bread…or serve as a side dish.

Penne with Tomato, Mozzarella and Basil

½ pound penne
4 Roma tomatoes, large diced
½ cup red onion, finely chopped
1 garlic clove (approximately 2 teaspoons very finely minced)
2 tablespoons dry white wine or Champagne vinegar
2 tablespoons olive oil, extra virgin
½ cup fresh basil, roughly chopped
½ teaspoon oregano, fresh
3 ounces mozzarella cheese, cut into small cubes
Salt, preferably Napastyle® gray salt
Pepper, freshly ground

At home:

Prepare the pasta per instructions on package for *al dente*.

Drain.

Rinse in cold water.

Add all the ingredients to drained pasta, except salt and pepper.

Toss lightly.

Salt and pepper to taste.

Refrigerate.

On boat:

For a quick salad, serve with crusty bread…or serve as a side dish.

Recommended wine:

Trezzi White Rooster Sauvignon Blanc
Lindemans® Pinot Noir

Potato Salad French Style

1 pound small white new potatoes
1 pound small red new potatoes
2 tablespoons dry white wine
2 tablespoons chicken or vegetable stock
Vinaigrette #4 (See Butters/Dressings/Oils/Vinaigrettes)
¼ cup scallion, both green and white parts, minced
2 tablespoons dill, fresh
2 tablespoons parsley, minced
2 tablespoons thyme leaves, minced
Salt
Pepper

Boil washed potatoes in salted water until cooked (about 20 minutes) and fork-tender.

NOTE: Do *not* overcook your potatoes.

Drain potatoes.

Let potatoes set until cool enough to handle.

Halve or quarter cooked potatoes (depending upon size).

Toss with wine and chicken (or vegetable) stock, allowing warm potatoes to absorb the liquid.

Make vinaigrette #4.

Add vinaigrette #4 to potatoes.

Toss with scallions, dill, parsley, thyme.

Salt and Pepper to taste.

Serve at room temperature.

STRAWBERRY SPINACH SALAD

1 pound spinach
1½ to 2 cups sliced strawberries
½ cup slivered almonds or candied walnuts
Vinaigrette #5 (See Butters/Dressings/Oils/Vinaigrettes)

Combine all of the above.

Toss.

NOTE: You can use store-bought raspberry vinaigrette, poppy-seed dressing, or any other dressing of your choice, although we think "sweet" dressings work best with this.

RECOMMENDED WINE:

Latah Creek May Wine

Unbelievable Shrimp Salad

WARNING: DON'T PUT THIS SALAD TOGETHER UNTIL YOU'RE READY TO SERVE IT ON THE BOAT. KEEP ALL INGREDIENTS COLD AT ALL TIMES. THE SHRIMP SHOULD BE ON ICE IN YOUR "FISH" COOLER.

2 pound jumbo shrimp in their shells (16-20 per pound)
3 tablespoons salt
1 lemon, quartered
½ cup red onion, finely minced (refrigerate)
1 ½ cup celery, minced (refrigerate)

Dressing

1 cup mayonnaise
½ teaspoon Dijon mustard
1 tablespoon white wine vinegar (or white wine)
½ teaspoon Napastyle ® gray salt
½ teaspoon pepper, preferably freshly grated
3 tablespoons dill, preferably fresh and minced.

At Home:

Prepare a large bowl of ice water.

Boil five quarts of water, 3 tablespoons of salt, and lemon quarters.

Add the shrimp.

Reduce heat to medium.

Cook uncovered for 3 minutes.

NOTE: This salad is best if the shrimp is slightly under-cooked.

Remove shrimp from boiling water with a slotted spoon and put into a bowl of ice water.

Cool.

When cooled, peel and de-vein.

Immediately refrigerate, on ice, and covered.

NOTE: We've discovered that the best way of icing peeled and de-veined shrimp to keep it from getting water-logged, is to put the shrimp in a Ziploc® bag, or airtight container, and then put that in a container of ice.

Refrigerate.

Shrimp Salad Dressing (keep separate until boat):

Make the dressing combining mayonnaise and mustard.

Whisk in vinegar (or white wine).

Add salt.

Add pepper.

Add dill.

Refrigerate.

On Boat:

Just before serving, combine the shrimp with Dressing.

Add the onion.

Add the celery.

Taste for seasoning.

Serve immediately.

NOTE: Immediately refrigerate or discard leftovers.

Recommended wine:

Overbluff Cellars "Vixen" Vognier

UNBELIEVABLE SHRIMP SALAD WITH PENNE

Follow our directions for **Unbelievable Shrimp Salad** (see above), BUT increase the mayonnaise to 1½ cups AND substitute large shrimp (25-30 per pound).

Just before serving, add 1 pound penne pasta that has been prepared ahead of time *al dente*, drained, tossed with olive oil, cooled, and refrigerated in an airtight container or Ziploc® bag.

NOTE: Do not refrigerate any pasta until it has thoroughly cooled.

Adjust seasoning, if needed.

RECOMMENDED WINE:

Overbluff Cellars "Vixen" Vognier

FISH AND SEAFOOD

WILLIAM—

As an avid cook, avid boater, avid fisherman, I'm never more satisfied, overjoyed, and downright pleased-as-punch, as when I'm able to combine those three pastimes by serving up, on my boat, some wondrously marvelous evening meal of the very fish, or fishes, caught fresh by me, or by one, or more, of my guests, from the lake, river, or ocean on which we sailed that day. While I existed contentedly for literally years, thinking that was the very same lifestyle appreciated by each and every boater on the world's waterways, it turns out I was wrong.

My co-author is, as are a good many boaters, many of them (dare I mention?) of the fairer sex, an exception to the rule that a good time on the water entails the presence of any kind of fishing pole, hook, slimy bait, eventual can't-get-any-fresher-than-this fish yanked from the water minutes before, cleaned, slapped on the hot grill, and eaten, with a lot of lip-smacking, at the end of day.

"No way!" says Bonnie, who can and does relate more than one horrible incident of a rocking boat, fish guts, and scales all over the place. "The scales are the worst! We were picking them up until the end of one boating season, usually one by one, between forefinger and thumb, tweezers-like. Never, never again!"

So, while my wider repertoire of fish recipes will have to be held onto for another day—BACK OF THE BOAT JUST-FISH COOKING (?)—I have managed to squeeze in a couple in this book; Bonnie, too, who, after all, has nothing against bringing already cleaned fish to the boat from home, has also graciously chipped in.

CATCH OF THE DAY

1 whole Catch of the Day: Trout, Silver Salmon, Bass, about 1 or 2 pounds, scaled and gutted
Olive oil
Salt, Kosher
Pepper, freshly ground
1 tablespoon lemon zest
1 lemon, thinly sliced

Preheat grill to high.

Well oil grate (be sure!)

Season fish well with the salt, pepper and the lemon zest, outside and in the cavity.

Put a few lemon slices in the cavity.

Brush the fish with oil.

Put fish on the grill.

Cook until slightly charred, about 3 to 5 minutes depending on the size of the fish.

Using wide spatula, carefully turn the fish and cook 4 to 7 minutes more, with lid of grill closed, until cooked thoroughly.

To serve, use a sharp knife to cut down the backbone of the fish and carefully remove the back bone, sliding the knife under the bones as you lift out.

Serve immediately.

NOTE: WATCH FOR BONES WHILE EATING!

RECOMMENDED WINE:

Lone Canary Pinot Grigio

H‍ERB-G‍RILLED S‍HRIMP

Wooden or metal 12-inch skewers

NOTE: Whenever using wooden skewers, soak them in water for at least ½ hour before using.

3 garlic cloves, finely minced
1 small onion, finely diced
¼ cup parsley, fresh, minced
¼ cup basil, fresh, minced
½ teaspoon dry mustard
2½ teaspoons Dijon mustard
2 teaspoons salt, preferably Kosher
¼ teaspoon pepper
¼ cup olive oil
Juice of one lemon
2 pound jumbo shrimp (16-20 per pound), peeled, except for tails, and de-veined.

At Home:

Mix together all ingredients, except the shrimp, to make marinade.

NOTE: The lemon juice will start to cook the shrimp so do not immediately start marinating, or shrimp will end up mushy when grilled.

NOTE: If transporting to your boat, be sure to keep in your fish cooler on ice at all times.

On Boat:

Marinate the Shrimp for about 30 minutes before grilling.

Preheat your grill on high.

Well oil grate.

Put shrimp on skewers (up to six shrimp per skewer makes for easier turning).

Grill for 1½ minutes.

Turn grilled shrimp.

Grill on other side for 1½ minutes.

Serve immediately.

NOTE: These can be used on a salad, with a Dijon vinaigrette, or in a Caesar salad...as an appetizer, by themselves or with dipping sauce...on pizza...or any number of other ways.

RECOMMENDED WINE:

Wawawai Canyon Winery Sangiovese

Oysters

NOTE (IMPORTANT): Ice, ice, ice! Always keep well-iced in your "fish" cooler any and all oysters in their shells until they're ready to use. By law, oysters in their shells must be sold live. Live oysters will be clamped tightly shut, or they will clamp tightly shut if tapped. Dead oysters will have loose shells and must be discarded. Also, discard any with broken shells. Buy as fresh as possible and use immediately.

36 large fresh oysters in their shells
Melted butter
Hot sauce (your favorite)
Lemon wedges

Scrub the oyster shells under cold running water with a brush, discarding any open or broken shells that indicate the oysters are dead and non-edible.

Preheat the grill on high.

Place oysters (cup-side down) on hot grill.

Close lid and cook 8-10 minutes or until the first shell opens (depending upon oyster size).

NOTE: If all shells do not open at the same time as the first one, those that don't will require prying open with an oyster knife or screwdriver. While prying the shells, be sure to use a mitten or towel to protect your hand. On the boat, you will want to do this sitting down. Cut the muscle that connects the upper and lower part of the shell, leaving the oyster on a half-shell, and be careful that you salvage and don't spill any of the juice.

Serve with melted butter, your favorite hot sauce, and lemon wedges.

Makes 6 servings.

RECOMMENDED WINE:

Nodland Cellars Bebop
Arbor Crest Wine Cellars Sparkling Wine

SALMON

SALMON ON CEDAR PLANK

Purchase cedar planks made for grilling. Do not use cedar shakes as they are usually treated with chemicals. Use only untreated cedar. One 10"-x-12" plank fits nicely on the Back of the Boat grill. Soak planks for at least 1 hour before using.

12-16 ounce piece of salmon, with skin on
Oil
Lemon pepper
Salt

Preheat grill to medium high.

Place plank on grill.

Oil the salmon on each side.

Sprinkle with salt and lemon pepper to taste.

Put salmon on plank.

Turn grill to medium-high.

Close the grill lid.

Grill for 12 to 15 minutes, depending on the thickness.

Check often.

Do not overcook.

NOTE: WATCH OUT FOR BONES WHILE EATING!

RECOMMENDED WINE:

Basalt Cellars Merlot
Goats do Roam Red/Classic Label
Whitestone Pieces of Red v. 6.022-
Liberty Lake Syrah

SALMON STEAKS WITH SPICE RUB

1 to 1½"-thick salmon steaks
Oil
2 lemons, halved
3 tablespoons coriander, whole
3 tablespoons cumin seeds, whole
3 tablespoons fennel seeds, whole
1 tablespoon black peppercorns
1 tablespoon sweet paprika
4 teaspoons of salt
½ to 1 teaspoon cayenne pepper
Dill and Cucumber Sauce (See Dips/Salsas/Sauces/Spreads)

At home:

Make Spice Rub—

In a small heavy skillet, toast the coriander, cumin, fennel, and peppercorns over medium heat, tossing or stirring frequently to toast evenly.

Spread toasted spices onto a plate to cool.

Put the cooled seeds in a blender, or for best results, in a coffee grinder.

Grind spices, finely.

Put finely ground spices into a bowl.

Add paprika, salt, and cayenne pepper.

Mix well.

Store in airtight container.

NOTE: Will keep for about 4 months in normal storage. In freezer, it will keep for about 1 year.

On boat:

Preheat grill to high.

Oil the grill, being sure it's well-oiled.

Brush both sides of the salmon with oil and season with the spice rub.

Grill for about 3 or 4 minutes. The salmon will "tell you" when it is ready to turn by allowing you to pull it away from the grate easily.

Turn salmon and continue to cook for another 3 or 4 minutes.

NOTE: Remember, fish continues to cook after it's removed from the heat, so it's is better to take it off a little too soon than too late. Once the "white" appears on the top you have overcooked it!

Brush lemon halves with oil.

Grill lemon halves, cut-side down until slightly charred.

Serve lemon and grilled salmon immediately with…

Dill and Cucumber Sauce.

RECOMMENDED WINE:

Barrister Winery Rough Justice

Salmon/Shrimp/Crab Cakes or "Burgers"

NOTE: This is a good way to use up leftover salmon or shrimp which you can even combine. These can be made ahead of time and refrigerated. They can be made small to serve as an appetizer, or they can be made bun-size for delicious fish burgers.

¼ to ⅓ cup mayonnaise
1 egg
3 tablespoons lemon juice, fresh
1½ teaspoon red bell pepper, finely minced
1½ teaspoon green onion, finely minced
1 teaspoon Old Bay® Seasoning
1 pound crab (cooked salmon, shrimp, or any combination thereof), drained if needed
1 to 1¼ cup Panko bread crumbs, plus extra to coat patties

Combine the first 6 ingredients and mix well.

Add the drained crab, salmon, or shrimp, mix well.

Add Panko crumbs, working with your hands until the mixture forms a ball that holds together.

Make cakes or patties.

Bread cakes or patties with additional Panko crumbs.

Refrigerate.

NOTE: These can be cooked on an oiled grill, or in a slightly oiled skillet on the grill.

Cook through, about 3 or 4 minutes per side.

Serve with flavored Mayonnaise (See Dips/Salsas/Sauces/Spreads)

Makes 4 patties or cakes…or about 8 appetizers.

RECOMMENDED WINE:

For shrimp and/or crab cakes: Latah Creek Chardonnay
For salmon cakes: Barili Cellars "Barrelin' Red"

MEAT

Burgers

The best ground-beef for cooking Back of the Boat is lean chuck or sirloin. A fatty ground burger, while juicer and tastier, provides grease flare-ups that you don't need on any boat! Suitable alternatives for beef, of course, are ground chicken or turkey. And a particular favorite of ours is ground buffalo.

To provide missing moisture, and to add flavor, mix in a splash of wine. Just for moisture, you can add a splash of water, too. Also, you can mold the meat around an ice cube, or around a frozen pat of flavored Butter (See Butters/Dressings/Oils/Vinaigrettes), either of which, as it melts, will add its moisture to the meat.

Inside-Out Burgers

Some people make these by stuffing the cheese, etc., between two patties. While that's certainly one way of doing it, these burgers take a long time to cook and usually result in their stuffing oozing out and burning on the grill and generally making a mess. We recommend mixing all of your supplemental ingredients (whatever you usually put *on* your burger, except for the lettuce) *into* the burger itself.

1½ pounds of ground meat, depending on how big a burger you enjoy
½ cup grated Swiss cheese
¼ pound bacon, chopped, and cooked to crisps
½ cup red onion, minced
2 tablespoons good red wine or water
¼ cup pickle, diced
1 large round Farmer's Bread (See Bread/Buns…from Round-Loaf Bread)

Combine all the ingredients, except the bread.

Mix lightly but well.

NOTE: To save space on the grill, we often form two big burgers, each of a suitable size to fit the bread we're using for the bun.

Preheat grill to high.

Well oil grate.

Turn grill to medium-high.

Grill for 4 to 5 minutes on each side, grill lid down, or until cooked as desired.

Insert into bun and cut appropriately for serving.

Serve immediately with Mustard Sauce (See Dips/Salsas/Sauces/Spreads), lettuce and tomato.

NOTE: You can, also, form the meat into 4 (still quite large) to 8 patties, and use regular Kaiser rolls, onion rolls, or regular hamburger buns. For these smaller patties, we like to use a wide-mouth mayonnaise-jar lid. Just line the lid with a piece of plastic wrap and form the patties in the lid. This way, your burgers will all be of uniform size. If someone wants a bigger burger, they can always have two patties.

NOTE: You can make the patties the night before if you just keep them well refrigerated.

RECOMMENDED WINE:

Townshend Cellar Cabernet Sauvignon

INSIDE-OUT BLEU-CHEESE BUFFALO BURGERS

1½ pound ground beef or buffalo
4 ounces Bleu Cheese, crumbled
1 cup French's French Fried Onions
3 or 4 pepperoncinis, minced
2 tablespoons wine or water
Jalapeño Focaccia Bread (See Bread/Buns...from Long-Loaf Bread).

Preheat grill to high.

Well oil grill.

Combine all the ingredients, except the bread.

Mix lightly but well.

NOTE: To save space on the grill, we often form two big burgers, each of a suitable size to fit the bread we're using for the bun.

Turn grill to medium-high.

Grill burgers for 3 to 4 minutes on each side, with the grill lid closed.

Insert into bun.

Cut for serving.

Serve immediately with whatever condiments, and lettuce, you didn't include in the making

NOTE: You can, also, form the meat into from 4 (still quite large) to 8 patties, and use regular Kaiser rolls onion rolls, or regular hamburger buns. For these smaller patties, we like to use a wide-mouth mayonnaise-jar lid. Just line the lid with a piece of plastic wrap and form the patties in the lid. This way, your burgers will all be of uniform size. If someone wants a bigger burger, they can always have two patties.

NOTE: You can make the patties the night before if you just keep them well refrigerated.

RECOMMENDED WINE:

Grande Ronde Cellars "Cellar Red"
Whitestone Winery Lake Roosevelt Red
Townshend Cellars Malbec

INSIDE-OUT SWISS MUSHROOM BURGERS

Onion rolls
1½ pound ground meat (your choice)
¼ pound crimini (baby portabella) mushrooms, roughly chopped
4 ounces Swiss cheese, grated
Salt and pepper, to taste

Preheat grill to high.

Well oil grate.

Grill halved onion rolls on grill until slightly toasted.

Remove rolls from grill and keep them warm

Mix all other ingredients lightly but well.

Form mixture into patties.

Grill patties to desired doneness.

Place patties between toasted onion-roll halves.

Serve immediately with lettuce and condiments of choice.

RECOMMENDED WINE:

…with chicken or turkey burgers: Ravenswood Winery Zinfandel
…with buffalo or beef burgers: Barrister Winery Cabernet Franc

INSIDE-OUT TACO BURGERS

1½ pound ground meat (your choice)
1 small red onion, finely diced
1 tablespoon cumin, ground
1 teaspoon dried oregano
1 small can mild to hot Jalapeño peppers, diced
2 tablespoons wine or water
Avocado slices, optional
Shredded lettuce
Shredded Cheddar and/or Monterey Jack cheese
Sour cream
Pico de Gallo (See Dips/Salsas/Sauces/Spreads)
Jalapeño Focaccia Bread (See (See Bread/Buns…from Long-Loaf Bread)
Corn chips
Guacamole (See Dips/Salsas/Sauces/Spreads)

Preheat grill to high.

Well oil grill.

Combine the first 6 ingredients.

Mix lightly but mix well.

NOTE: To save space on the grill, we often form two big burgers, each of a suitable size to fit the bread we're using for the bun.

Turn grill to medium-high.

Grill the burgers, grill lid down, for 4 to 5 minutes on each side, or until cooked as desired.

Insert into bun.

Cut appropriately for serving.

Serve with Pico de Gallo, avocado slices, cheese, shredded lettuce, and dollop of sour cream, with corn chips, and Guacamole on the side.

NOTE: By way of a shortcut, use an envelope of dry taco mix in place of spices.

NOTE: You can form the meat into 4 (still quite large) to 8 patties, and use regular Kaiser rolls, onion rolls, or regular hamburger buns. For these smaller patties, we like to use a wide-mouth mayonnaise-jar lid. Just line the lid with a piece of plastic wrap and form the patties in the lid. This way, your burgers will all be of uniform size. If someone wants a bigger burger, they can always have two patties.

You can make the patties the night before if you just keep them well refrigerated.

Beef Steak

Rib-Eye

2 pound boneless rib-eye, 1½"-2" thick
Montreal Steak Seasoning

Take steak out of refrigerator or cooler at least 30 minutes before grilling.

Preheat grill to high.

Well oil grate.

Sprinkle meat generously with Montreal Steak Seasoning.

Put on grill.

For medium rare: When juice start to rise to the top of the steak, about 7 to 8 minutes, turn steak. For rare or well done, adjust time accordingly

Cook for another 7 to 8 minutes.

Remove from grill.

Cover and let rest for 10 to 15 minutes.

NOTE: Steak continues to cook as it rests.

Carve in ½" slices.

Serve immediately.

Serves 4, or 2 with leftovers for sandwiches with Horseradish Mayonnaise (See Dips/Salsas/Sauces/Spreads)

<u>**RECOMMENDED WINE:**</u>

Nodland Cellars Reserve Cabernet Sauvignon
Chiarello Family Vineyards Roux Old Vine Petite Sirah
Grande Ronde Cellars Charlotte's Cuvee
Townshend Cellars Reserve
Whitestone Winery Cabernet Sauvignon

HAM

GLAZED HAM

1½ pound Ham steak, cut 1½"-2" thick
6 tablespoons Dijon mustard
3 tablespoons honey
1 tablespoon horseradish

Prepare glaze by whisking all ingredients, except ham.

NOTE: Glaze can be made ahead of time, covered, and refrigerated, BUT bring back to room temperature before using.

Preheat the grill to high.

Well oil grate.

Brush the ham with glaze and put on grill.

Close grill lid and lower heat to medium.

Grill 9-10 minutes on each side, basting with glaze every few minutes, until the ham is cooked thoroughly.

Remove ham from grill.

Brush ham with more glaze.

Let ham rest for 5 minutes.

Carve into 1" slices.

Serve immediately.

Serves 4.

Serve with Green Eggs (See Eggs)

RECOMMENDED WINE:

Xomosa (See DRINK)

GLAZED HAM WITH PINEAPPLE

1½ pound ham steak, 1½"-2" thick
1 cup apricot preserves
¼ cup brown sugar
3 tablespoons of pineapple juice
1 pineapple, fresh, peeled, cored, sliced into ½" slices ahead of time

At home:

Prepare glaze by mixing apricot preserve, brown sugar, and pineapple juice.

NOTE: If glaze is too thick, add a teaspoon or so of water to thin.

On boat:

Brush glaze on ham and on pineapple slices.

Set pineapple slices aside.

Put ham slices on grill.

Turn grill to medium, and grill ham for 8-10 minutes on each side, brushing with glaze every few minutes.

When ham is nicely glazed and heated through, remove from heat.

Brush more glaze on the ham and let it rest for about 5 minutes.

Grill pineapple slices, brushing each side (about 2 minutes for each side).

Carve ham into 1" slices and serve immediately with pineapple slices, the later cut in half.

RECOMMENDED WINE:

Latah Creek Riesling
Dutch Henry Napa Valley Chardonnay

Hot Dogs

Breakfast Dogs

NOTE: This is a great recipe for kids and grown-ups alike. Try it with catsup and mustard, even hot sauce! You might be pleasantly surprised at how good it tastes on eggs early in the morning, your boat anchored in a quiet little bay. You need only accompany with some fresh orange juice or fresh fruit and cup of fresh brewed espresso.

Hot dogs or sausage, any you prefer, whole or sliced
Eggs
Cheese, your choice
Condiments, of the usual variety used for hot dogs

Preheat grill to high.

Preheat frying pan on the grill for eggs.

Put the hot dogs on the grill.

Put eggs in frying pan, one at a time and break yolks.

Turn each egg over and top with a piece of cheese.

NOTE: Bruce prefers pepperjack cheese. William loves sharp cheddar. Bonnie prefers any mild cheese.

As hot dogs and eggs cook, grill buns and set them aside.

NOTE: If you don't have enough room on the grill for everything, start out with grilling the buns and then set them aside, covered with foil, to keep them warm; the eventual addition of hot dog and cheese will soften a bun.

Put an egg with melted cheese on each bun and top with hot dog.

Dress with condiments of your choice.

RIBS

COUNTRY RIBS

NOTE: Best if prepared the day before.

4 pounds country-style ribs
Salt and pepper
Spicy Barbecue Sauce (See Dips/Salsas/Sauces/Spreads)

At home:

Salt and pepper ribs.

Brown ribs in large frying pan on stove.

Remove ribs to Crock-Pot®.

Prepare Spicy Barbecue Sauce in same frying pan as used for browning.

Cover ribs in Crock-Pot® with Spicy Barbecue Sauce.

Cook Crock-Pot® on high for 1 to 1½ hours, until tender.

Let Crock-Pot® cooked ribs cool.

Remove ribs from Crock-Pot®.

Place ribs in an airtight container or Ziploc® bag with sauce.

Refrigerate until ready for transport to boat.

On boat:

Preheat grill to high.

Well oil grate.

Remove ribs from container and/or Ziploc® bag or bags.

Put ribs on grill.

Close grill lid.

Cook ribs about 5 minutes on each side. Don't overheat, or they'll be dry. We sometimes place a piece of foil lightly over the top of the cooking meat to keep in the moisture and make them cook faster.

Heat any leftover sauce in a pan on the grill and serve on the side; yes, the sauce will be okay to eat, because the ribs and it are already thoroughly cooked.

Recommended wine:

Wawawai Canyon Winery Rosé
Dutch Henry Napa Valley Reserve Estate Cabernet Sauvignon
Townshend Cellars Lemberger
Abacela Cabernet Franc
Whitestone Winery Cabernet Franc

POULTRY (CHICKEN)

BRIAN'S HOT WINGS

CAUTION: These...ARE... HOT!

4 pounds chicken wings, fresh
2 twelve-ounce bottles Frank Red Hot Sauce®
1 package Buffalo Wing Screaming Hot Seasoning Mix
1 package Buffalo Wing Cajun Seasoning Mix
1 teaspoon Italian Seasoning
1 teaspoon horseradish
1 teaspoon cayenne pepper
1 teaspoon brown sugar
2 tablespoons red wine
3 tablespoons juice from pepperoncinis, OR 2 tablespoons vinegar
10 drops Tabasco® sauce
1 tablespoon bread crumbs

At home:

Preheat oven to 350F.

Combine all ingredients, except the chicken wings, in a bowl.

Mix well.

Remove tips from chicken wings, and cut at joints.

Divide wings into the cooking bags that come with the seasoning mixes.

Divide the sauce, pour over wings in the bags.

Bake according to directions on seasoning package.

Remove from oven.

Remove wings from bag and cool in the refrigerator, in a single layer on a cookie sheet immediately.

Cool sauce and put in airtight container.

Put cooled wings in an airtight container or Ziploc®.

Refrigerate.

At boat:

Preheat grill to high.

Well oil grill.

Heat sauce in pan on grill.

Using tongs, dip wings in sauce and put on grill.

Grill until heated through and slightly charred.

Dip wings in sauce again and serve with bleu cheese Dressing (See Dips/Salsas/Sauces/Spreads)…or with a sprinkling of bleu cheese…and celery sticks.

RECOMMENDED WINE:

Barrister Winery Riesling

Other beverage of choice:

Ice-cold beer (brand of your choice)

FIESTA TEQUILA LIME CHICKEN

¼ cup Cuervo Gold Tequila®
½ cup lime juice, preferably fresh-squeezed
¼ cup orange juice, preferably fresh-squeezed
1½ teaspoons chili powder
1 tablespoon jalapeño pepper, minced
2 garlic cloves, minced
1½ teaspoon cilantro, optional
1 teaspoon salt, Kosher
½ teaspoon pepper, freshly ground
4 split boneless chicken breasts, skin on

At home:

Combine all the ingredients except salt, pepper, and the chicken, for the marinade.

Mix well.

Put chicken in a Ziploc® bag.

Pour marinate over chicken.

Refrigerate overnight.

On boat:

Preheat grill to medium high.

Well oil grate.

Salt and pepper breasts.

Put breasts skin-side down on grill.

Grill until skin is brown, about 5-6 minutes.

Turn and grill for about 10 minutes more.

Move to a platter and cover tightly with foil.

Let cooked chicken rest for at least 5 minutes.

Serve hot, or at room temperature.

RECOMMENDED WINE:

Lindemans® Pinot Noir
Townshend Cellar Sauvignon Blanc
Townshend Cellar Chardonnay

Marinated Grilled Lemon Chicken

½ cup lemon juice, preferably fresh-squeezed, about 2 lemons
½ cup olive oil
1 teaspoons Napastyle® gray salt
½ teaspoon pepper, freshly ground
2 teaspoons thyme leaves, minced
2 boneless, skinless chicken breasts, halved

At home:

Combine all the ingredients except the chicken.

Pour over chicken in a Ziploc® bag.

Refrigerate for at least 6 hours.

On boat:

Preheat grill to medium high.

Well oil grate.

Grill breasts about 10 minutes on each side.

Remove from grill.

Cool slightly.

Cut diagonally into ½" slices.

Serve on a salad…on a pizza…in a pita…or in a wrap.

NOTE: For faster cooking time, butterfly the breasts before marinating. They will be thinner and will cook faster, about 3-5 minutes each side.

PASTA

Never try to cook pasta on your grill. Firstly, you will never get water to boil, and you will always end up with a gluey mess. Secondly, a big pot of hot water on a rocking boat can be very dangerous. Cook pasta not all of the way to *al dente*) beforehand, and reheat it, on board, in whatever your sauce.

CLAMS WITH **L**INGUINE

1 tablespoon salt, preferably Kosher
¼ cup olive oil
1 tablespoon garlic, minced
¼ teaspoon red pepper, crushed
½ cup white dry vermouth or a good white wine
24 little-neck clams, rinsed and scrubbed
¼ teaspoon minced lemon zest
1 pound linguine
2 teaspoons basil, fresh, chopped
2 tablespoons flat-leaf parsley, fresh, chopped
Crusty bread slices (of your choice)

At home:

Prepare pasta, following the directions on the package for *al dente*, BUT slightly undercook; it will cook more as it's reheated in sauce.

Put a cup of pasta water to one side to take with you to the boat.

Drain remaining cooked pasta.

Rinse cooked pasta in cold water.

Drizzle drained pasta lightly with olive oil and toss.

Put cooled and oiled pasta in a Ziploc® bag or airtight container.

Refrigerate.

Take to boat.

<u>On boat:</u>

Preheat grill to medium.

In large skillet, gently heat the oil, minced garlic, and red-pepper flakes, until the garlic sizzles and just begins to turn brown.

Add vermouth or wine and bring to boil.

Add clams and lemon zest.

Turn grill to high.

Cover to steam the clams 4-5 minutes.

When the clams just begin to open, add parsley and basil.

Continue to cook clams, stirring until they've all fully opened.

Remove from heat.

Add pasta.

Add pasta water, if needed, to thin or increase sauce.

Toss lightly.

Serve with slices of crusty bread to sop up the juices.

RECOMMENDED WINE:

Lone Canary Pinot Grigio

HERB PASTA

1 pound spaghetti
4 tablespoons olive oil
3 cloves garlic, minced
½ cup Italian parsley and curly parsley, roughly chopped
2 tablespoons fresh chives, finely chopped
1 teaspoon thyme leaves, fresh
1 lemon (for juice)
1 teaspoon lemon zest
Parmigiano Reggiano or Parmesan cheese
1½ cup shredded cooked or grilled chicken or shrimp.
Grilled Veggies, optional (See Vegetables)

At home:

Prepare pasta, following the directions on the package for *al dente*, BUT slightly undercook; it will cook more once it's reheated with the sauce.

Put a cup of pasta water to one side to take with you to the boat.

Drain remaining cooked pasta.

Rinse cooked pasta in cold water.

Drizzle drained pasta lightly with olive oil and toss.

Put cooled and oiled pasta in a Ziploc® bag or airtight container.

Refrigerate.

On boat:

Preheat a sauté pan on the grill over medium heat.

Add 4 tablespoons of olive oil.

Turn the grill on low and add garlic.

Sauté until golden (about 2 minutes)

Add the pasta and enough pasta water to make a sauce that isn't watery.

Squeeze in juice from half a lemon.

Add 1 teaspoon of lemon zest.

Remove from grill.

Add rest of ingredients.

Toss lightly.

RECOMMENDED WINE:

Robert Karl Cellars Sauvignon Blanc

BREAD

Bruschetta

Bruschetta can be topped with just about anything you can think up. It is usually made with a French bread, baguette, or similar Italian bread. It is perfect with a glass of good wine, and maybe a salad, but the bruschetta can be very filling and therefore becomes light dinner or lunch, all on its own.

Bruschetta with Apricot Jam or Orange Marmalade

Ciabatta Bread sliced ½" thick, about 12 slices
15- or 16-ounce carton of ricotta cheese
¾ cup apricot jam or orange marmalade

Preheat grill to medium high.

Grill bread to golden brown on each side.

Spread about 2 tablespoons of ricotta cheese on each piece of toast and top with 1 tablespoon of jam or marmalade.

Bruschetta with Classic Tomato Basil Topping

4 Roma tomatoes, diced
½ cup red onion, finely chopped

2 garlic cloves (about 2 teaspoons, very finely minced)
1 tablespoon balsamic vinegar, plus more for drizzling on top or dipping
½ cup fresh basil, roughly chopped
1 teaspoon oregano, fresh
Salt, preferably Napastyle® gray salt
Pepper, freshly ground
Bread (of your choice)
Garlic clove
Olive oil

Combine tomatoes, onion, minced garlic clove, balsamic vinegar, basil, oregano, salt and pepper, for Classic Tomato Basil Topping.

Toss lightly.

Cover and refrigerate.

Prepare bread by cutting it lengthwise.

NOTE: This is easier than having your grill covered with lots of individual bread pieces.

Grill bread with cut-surfaces, face-down, until toasted.

Rub garlic clove on cut bread surfaces and brush same with olive oil.

Cut into 2½" slices.

Top each slice with approximately 2 tablespoons of Classic Tomato Basil Topping.

Drizzle with balsamic vinegar (and olive oil, if desired). Serve immediately.

NOTE: We sometimes merely pile the prepared bread on a board or platter and serve separately the Classic Tomato Basil Topping, the balsamic vinegar, and the olive oil.

NOTE: If you have guests, use two bowls of the Tomato Basil Topping, one on each end of the board or platter, with several spoons so your guests can serve themselves.

BRUSCHETTA WITH GRILLED FRESH ASPARAGUS AND CHEESE

1 loaf French bread or bread of your choice
2 garlic cloves
Olive oil
Salt, preferably Napastyle® gray salt
1¼ pounds large asparagus spears (the larger have more flavor and are easier to handle on the grill)
8-ounce Fontina or Monterey Jack cheese, fresh, grated
2-ounce Parmesan cheese, fresh, grated

At home:

Cut the tough ends from the asparagus spears.

Peel the asparagus spears.

Toss the asparagus spears with olive oil and one garlic clove, minced.

Put asparagus spears in Ziploc® bag, along with marinade.

Refrigerate.

On the boat:

Preheat the grill to high.

Well oil grate.

Cut bread in half, lengthwise.

Brush olive oil on cut bread surfaces.

Turn grill to medium.

Put bread, cut-sides down, on grill.

Toast bread on grill, cut-sides down.

Remove bread from grill.

Rub toasted sides of bread with garlic, and brush or drizzle with olive oil.

Grill the asparagus 3-4 minutes, turning frequently, until tender and slightly charred.

Turn the grill to low.

Sprinkle the Fontina cheese evenly on toasted sides of bread.

Arrange asparagus spears on top of cheese.

Sprinkle asparagus spears with Parmesan.

Grill on low heat, with the lid closed, until the cheese is melted and the bread brown, watching closely to prevent burning, especially if you don't "know" your grill.

NOTE: We will sometimes place a piece of foil loosely over the bread just to help the cheese melt faster.

Slice and serve.

BRUSCHETTA WITH NON-CLASSIC BRUSCHETTA TOPPING

Prepare bread as in **Bruschetta with Grilled Fresh Asparagus and Cheese** (See Above).

Top with…

Roasted Garlic and Eggplant Spread (available in 9-ounce jar).

Or with…

Muffuletta Mix (available in 8-ounce jar).

Or with...

Tapenade (available in 8-ounce jar).

Then, top with 1 cup diced tomatoes, minced red onion, if desired, and sprinkle with fresh basil, roughly chopped and shaved Parmesan cheese

Drizzle with, or dip into, olive oil and/or balsamic vinegar.

BRUSCHETTA FOR BREAKFAST

4 slices of rustic Italian bread
6 eggs
2 tablespoons water
½ teaspoon salt
1 tablespoons Tabasco® Sauce
1 tablespoon butter
3 ounces goat cheese, soft
1 tablespoon marinated sun-dried tomatoes, finely julienned
Basil leaves, fresh, chiffinade
Classic Pesto (See Dips/Salsas/Sauces/Spreads)

Preheat grill to medium high.

Grill bread to golden brown on each side and keep warm, while...

Prepare the eggs—

Heat skillet on grill.

Melt butter in skillet.

Whisk eggs, water, Tabasco®, and salt.

Pour whipped eggs into skillet.

Stir gently until eggs are scrambled.

Spread the toasted bread with the soften goat cheese.

Top goat cheese with scrambled eggs.

Garnish with the sun-dried tomatoes, basil, and drizzle with Pesto Sauce.

BUNS

Don't get stuck in the plain-old bun-rut. There are so many wonderful artisan breads on the market, today, that make fabulous "buns" for burgers. Use your imagination, improvise, and cut accordingly. If the bread is too fat, just split it lengthwise into 3-4 pieces. Use any leftover pieces for toast in the morning.

BUNS FROM LONG-LOAF BREAD

Preheat grill to medium.

Split any long-loaf artisan bread lengthwise. If the bread is really thick, you can split it into three long slices but save the middle slice for later, possibly to toast for breakfast.

Toast two halves, cut-sides down, on grill.

Slice into 2½"-3" slices to form the "buns."

BUNS FROM ROUND-LOAF BREAD

Preheat grill to medium.

Split any round-loaf artisan bread lengthwise into 3-4 pieces, depending upon thickness.

Save the middle piece(s) for breakfast.

Toast the remaining 2 pieces, cut-sides down, on grill.

NOTE: Jalapeño Bread, Herb Bread, and/or Garlic Fontana bread, are usually found in your grocery store, or deli, and are all wonderful accompaniments to eggs.

CROSTINI

Slice a baguette into ½" slices.
Brush one side of slice with oil.
Sprinkle with salt and pepper to taste.

At home:

Preheat conventional oven to 350 degrees.

Bake one side of slices on a greased cookie sheet for 10-15 minutes.

Turn slices.

Bake on second side until nicely brown and crisp.

Cool completely before serving or storing.

NOTE: These can be made ahead of time and kept in airtight containers for 2-3 days.

On boat:

Preheat grill to medium.

Warm crostinis, if desired.

NOTE: If you prefer to prepare these on the boat, you can do so on your grill by following the same procedure as you'd do at home, being sure to watch that your bread doesn't burn.

PIZZA

Pizza Dough

Make enough pizza dough for whatever the size pizza or pizzas you have in mind.

Don't panic. These recipes may seem long and complicated, but pizza dough is actually very easy to make

Feel free to use either the white-flour or a whole-wheat recipe. The latter, of course, is healthier for you, because of the nutrients not removed during the processing of the flour. It's the whole-wheat pizza that's usually most preferred by diners when we've presented them with a choice between the two. That said…you need merely rely upon your mood, at the moment, or on whether or not white- or whole- wheat flour is what you have immediately available.

By the way, we recommend you always keep your flour in the freezer, like we do, to kill any bugs. However, be sure to bring it out, and up to room temperature, before you use it.

If you have a bread machine, merely follow the manufacturer's instructions for pizza dough; we use a mixer with a dough hook, and it usually only takes a few minutes. If you don't have a bread machine, or don't want to take the time to make pizza dough from scratch, you can always buy frozen pizza dough in the grocery store…or in some parts of the country even directly from your local pizzeria. Whether your own dough, or had from somewhere else, feel free to mix with it whatever herbs, spices, and/or garlic that you personally think will make it more tasty for you.

PIZZA DOUGH WITH ALL-PURPOSE WHITE FLOUR

1 cup warm water (105° F to 115° F)
1 package dry yeast
1 teaspoon honey (or sugar)
3 cups of all-purpose flour
1 teaspoon salt, coarse
1 tablespoon basil, fresh, chopped, optional
1 garlic clove, finely minced, optional
1 tablespoon extra-virgin olive oil, or Garlic Oil (See Butters/Dressings/Oils/Vinaigrettes), plus more for brushing and drizzling, optional.

PIZZA DOUGH WITH WHOLE-WHEAT FLOUR

1 cup warm water (105° F to 115° F)
1 package dry yeast
1 teaspoon honey (or sugar)
½ teaspoon salt, coarse
1 teaspoon olive oil or Garlic Oil (See Butters/Dressings/Oils/Vinaigrettes)
1 tablespoon basil, fresh, chopped, optional
1 garlic clove, finely minced, optional
1⅓ cup whole-wheat flour
1⅓ cup all-purpose flour

If using a bread machine…

Follow the manufacturer's directions.

If using a mixer…

Dissolve the yeast and the honey (or sugar) in cup of warm water. Set aside. Eventually, it should start to bubble in indication that the yeast is active.

In a mixing bowl, combine the flour, basil, garlic, and salt, using dough hook.

Add the oil, or 1 tablespoon of Garlic Oil, the yeast mixture.

Mix on low speed for about 5 minutes, until dough comes away from the sides and gathers around the dough hook.

Turn the dough out onto a lightly floured surface and knead by hand for 2 or 3 minutes until dough is smooth and firm.

If you have time, let the dough rise in a warm spot, covered with a clean, damp towel for about 30 minutes, then punch down. If you don't have the time, go directly to the next step. Which is …

Divide the dough into 4 balls and put in oiled Ziploc® plastic bags. Put them in the cooler, during which they will rise a little but not much.

Take dough out of cooler. Let it rise for about 1-1½ hours, or until doubled.

Knead the dough, on a floured peel or bread board (about 2 minutes), and let it rest for at least 15 more minutes.

Scatter corn meal or flour over the flat surface of your pizza peel, to keep your dough from sticking. Then, either flatten or roll out your dough. If the dough has a tendency to shrink back, let it rests for an additional 10 minutes and try again.

Brush one side of flattened or rolled pizza dough with oil.

GRILLING PIZZA

Turn the grill to high.

Well oil your grate.

Slide dough from peel onto grill, oiled side down

Turn grill to medium.

Grill pizza dough until brown, on bottom, watching carefully, especially if you don't "know" your grill, because the dough can burn easily.

When the pizza dough is brown and bubbled, remove it from the grill, cooked side up, uncooked side down, and place on pizza peel.

To the cooked side of the pizza, pile on whatever pizza toppings you prefer (See Pizza/Toppings), and slide the pizza off the pizza peel to place the *uncooked* side down on the grill.

Close the grill lid, and watch closely until the topping is hot, and the crust is golden brown.

Remove from grill.

Drizzle with Garlic Oil, if desired.

Makes about 4 six-inch pizzas, or 2 oblong pizzas.

PIZZA TOPPINGS

There are so many ways to top a pizza.

Traditionally, it's topped with tomato sauce, pepperoni and mozzarella cheese.

RECOMMENDED WINE:

Trezzi Farm Estate Barbera
Whitestone Cabernet Franc

However, for those bored with predictable toppings, there is a variety of cheeses that are fabulous on pizza, besides mozzarella. We recommend you try Montrachet Goat Cheese, or Fontina, bleu cheese, feta, even cheddar, and cream cheese. Look in the gourmet section of any cheese aisle of any store or deli. Better yet, ask your cheese monger to recommend a cheese to you.

Sometimes, we go against tradition, all together, and don't use any cheese at all. Top your pizza with grilled veggies, fresh tomatoes, and fresh herbs, even a complete salad. Follow the directions **Grilling Pizza** (See Above).

Or…

Instead of tomato sauce, use Pesto (See Dips/Salsas/Sauces/Spreads) and goat cheese, following the directions for **Grilling Pizza** (See Above). Then, garnish with freshly sliced tomatoes, fresh basil (chiffonade), sprinkled with Napastyle® gray salt; all drizzled with oil.

RECOMMENDED WINE:

Merry Cellars Sauvignon Blanc

Or…

Brush on Garlic Oil, Chili Oil, or Garlic and Chili Oil (See Butters/Dressings/Oils/Vinaigrettes), even olive oil.

Top with tomatoes, spinach, feta cheese.

Follow with directions for **Grilling Pizza** (See Above)

Drizzle with even more oil.

Or…

Brush with Garlic and Chili Oil (See Butters/Dressings/Oils/Vinaigrettes).

Top with jarred artichokes, thinly sliced red onions, Niçoise olives, freshly grated Parmigiano Reggiano, and garnish with roughly chopped basil.

Follow directions for **Grilling Pizza** (See Above)

Drizzle with more Garlic and Chili Oil.

Or…

Grill both sides until crust is golden brown.

Brush with Garlic Oil (See Butters/Dressings/Oils/Vinaigrettes), and top with a Caesar Salad to which you can add grilled shrimp or grilled chicken.

Or…

Grill both sides until crust is golden brown.

Spread with Dill Cream Cheese Spread (See Dips/Salsas/Sauces/Spreads).

Top with thin slices of slices of red onion, smoked salmon, and a dollop of caviar.

RECOMMENDED WINE:

Mountain Dome Sparkling Wine
Kenwood Sparkling Wine
Veuve Clicquot Champagne

NOTE: Our favorite bought pizza toppings are the homemade pesto and marinara sauces we get from wonderfully Italian "Trezzi Farm Food and Wine," in our area [17700 N Dunn Rd, Green Bluff WA 99055, Phone: (509) 238-2276]. In a pinch, though, we've even purchased fresh pesto and marinara sauce from the gourmet section of our local grocery store.

NOTE: The best route to go, however, is to make your own sauces when the vegetables are in season; freeze them for later use.

DIPS/SALSAS/SAUCES/SPREADS

Classic Basil Pesto

3 tablespoons pine nuts
2 cups basil, fresh leaves, firmly packed
½ cup olive oil
½ teaspoon garlic, minced
Salt, preferably Napastyle® gray salt
Ascorbic acid, or Vitamin C powder (a pinch)
¼ cup freshly grated Parmesan cheese

Put the pine nuts in a dry pan, over medium heat.

Keep the pan moving until the nuts are just starting to turn brown.

Set pan and nuts aside to cool.

Have bowl of ice water handy.

Put the basil in a sieve or strainer and put into a pan of boiling water.

NOTE: Be sure the basil leaves are completely covered.

Stir boiling basil about 15 seconds, and then plunge them into ice water to cool quickly.

Drain the basil leaves immediately, squeezing out all of the water.

Roughly chop the basil.

In a blender, puree the basil with the olive oil, pine nuts, garlic, salt (to taste), and an pinch of the powdered ascorbic acid in a blender.

NOTE: Do not use a food processor; the blender does a far better job.

When blended, add the cheese until mixed.

Keep refrigerated until ready to use.

Makes about ¾ cup.

NOTE: We make as many batches as we have basil for, and then freeze it. Sometimes, with a bumper crop of basil, we will have enough to last us through the winter. Basil is easily grown, by the way, in the garden or in pots, and we recommend you give it a try. It likes hot weather and will die at the first sign of frost, though; so be prepared.

NOTE: Ascorbic Acid and/or Vitamin C not only keeps your pesto from turning brown, but provides an added little citric flavor. You can get it powdered in any health-food store. We just buy tablets, wherever vitamins are sold and use a mortar and pestle to powder the pills for whatever the pinch or two that's usually all that's required.

Dill and Cucumber Sauce

¾ cup sour cream
¾ cup mayonnaise
¾ cup cucumber, finely diced
4 scallions, white and green parts, finely minced
2 tablespoons parsley, finely minced
1 tablespoon dill, fresh, finely minced
1 teaspoon salt, Kosher
¾ teaspoon pepper, freshly ground

Combine all ingredients, except salt and pepper.

Mix well.

Salt and pepper to taste.

Refrigerate.

NOTE: Stir well before serving.

DILL CREAM CHEESE SPREAD

1 cup sour cream
8-ounce package cream cheese
3 tablespoons finely minced scallions
1½ tablespoons dill, minced
1 tablespoon lemon juice, freshly squeezed
Pepper, freshly ground

Combine all ingredients but pepper.

Mix well.

Pepper to taste.

Cover and refrigerate.

Keeps refrigerated for about a week.

NOTE: Use this with salmon, shrimp, or crab cake/burgers (See Fish and Seafood/Salmon/Shrimp/Crab Cakes or "Burgers").

GUACAMOLE

4-5 Haas avocados, halved, pitted, peeled, and diced (NOT mashed)
Juice of 1 lime, about 3 tablespoons
8-10 dashes of Tabasco® sauce
½ small red onion, finely chopped
1 garlic clove, finely minced
2 tablespoons cilantro leaves (optional), fresh, chopped
1 tomato, medium, seeded, small-diced
Salt, preferably Napastyle® gray salt
Pepper, freshly ground

Combine all ingredients, except for salt and pepper.

Toss well.

Salt and pepper to taste.

NOTE: You'll want this to be chunky, NOT mashed.

Serve at room temperature.

NOTE: This can be made a few hours ahead of time by pressing plastic wrap directly on top of the mixture, to seal it, and then refrigerating it.

WARNING: This does NOT keep well.

HERBED GOAT CHEESE SPREAD

8 ounces cream cheese, room temperature
10 ounces mild goat cheese, room temperature
2 garlic cloves, finely minced
½ teaspoon thyme leaves, fresh, minced
3 tablespoons parsley, fresh, minced
5-6 tablespoons half-and-half (milk will do in a pinch)
¾ teaspoon salt, Kosher
½ teaspoon pepper, freshly grated
English cucumber

Beat cream cheeses until smooth.

Add other ingredients, except salt and pepper, including just 5 tablespoons of half and half.

Mix well.

If too thick (should spread easily), add the additional 1 tablespoon of half and half.

Salt and pepper to taste.

Serve on crackers or Crostini (See Bread/Crostini).

Top with an English cucumber slice.

NOTE: This can also be used as a delicious sandwich spread.

MAYONNAISE

CHIPOTLE MAYONNAISE

1 cup mayonnaise
2 chipotles peppers in adobo sauce
1 tablespoon adobo sauce
2 tablespoons fresh lime juice
Salt and pepper

In a blender, puree all the ingredients.

Season to taste.

Refrigerate.

HORSERADISH MAYONNAISE

1 cup mayonnaise
2 tablespoons Dijon Whole Grain Mustard
¼ cup prepared horseradish, drained
Salt

Whisk together all ingredients but salt.

Salt to taste.

Refrigerate for at least 30 minutes before using, in order to blend flavors.

Wasabi Mayonnaise

1 cup mayonnaise
2 tablespoons wasabi, prepared
2 tablespoons soy sauce
1 teaspoon sugar

Whisk together all the ingredients until well mixed.

Refrigerate.

Mustard Sauce

⅔ cup mayonnaise
⅓ cup Dijon mustard
½ teaspoon Worcestershire Sauce
8-10 dashes of Tabasco®

Whisk all ingredients together.

Refrigerate.

Makes 1 cup.

NOTE: This will keep for a very long time, and we use it on just about anything and everything.

PICO DE GALLO

4 Roma tomatoes, seeded and diced
2 jalapeño peppers, finely diced
1 small red onion, finely diced
2 tablespoons of lime juice
½ teaspoon garlic, finely minced
½ cup cilantro leaves, loosely packed and roughly chopped
½-¾ teaspoon salt, preferably Napastyle® gray salt
Pepper, preferably freshly ground

Combine everything.

Mix.

Adjust seasoning to taste.

Place in air-tight container.

Serve immediately or refrigerate.

Makes 2-3 cups.

NOTE: Can be made up to two days in advance.

NOTE: You don't need do all the chopping on the boat, but can chop everything beforehand, at home, and bring it with you.

RECOMMENDED WINE:

Basalt Cellars Muscat Canelli

Quick-and-Easy Salsa

1 fourteen-ounce can tomatoes, petite diced
2 tablespoons red onion, finely diced
1 jalapeño, fresh, seeded and finely minced (or) 2 tablespoons diced canned jalapeños
1 tablespoon lime juice
3 tablespoons cilantro, fresh, chopped
½ teaspoon garlic, finely minced
Salt and pepper.

Combine all ingredients but salt and pepper.

Mix.

Salt and pepper to taste.

Place in an air-tight container.

Serve immediately or keep refrigerated.

Makes about 2 cups

NOTE: You can make this as much as two days ahead.

NOTE: This is a favorite of ours. We always have the ingredients for it on board for any quick get-together with friends, and/or just for snacking with corn chips, and/or just for perking up almost anything from breakfast eggs, to Bruschetta, to a main course, even pizza.

SMOKED SALMON SPREAD

8 ounces cream cheese, room temperature
½ cup sour cream
1 tablespoon lemon juice, preferably fresh
1 tablespoon fresh dill, minced
1 tablespoon chives, finely chopped
1 tablespoon scallions, finely diced
1 teaspoon horseradish, drained
½ teaspoon salt, preferably Kosher
¼ teaspoon black pepper, freshly ground
4 ounces salmon, smoked and minced

In a mixer, using the paddle attachment, cream the cheese until smooth.

Add all the ingredients, except the salmon, salt and pepper.

Mix well.

Add the salmon.

Mix well.

Salt and pepper to taste.

Refrigerate.

Serve with crackers, crudités, or Crostini (See Breads/ Crostini).

RECOMMENDED WINE:

Villa Castegas Zinfandel
Château Jacques Blanc St. Émilion Grand Cru Cuvée du Maître

Spicy Barbecue Sauce

2 tablespoons oil
1 onion, medium, diced
1 eight-ounce can tomato sauce
½ cup brown sugar, packed
¼ cup white vinegar
1 tablespoon Worcestershire Sauce
4 teaspoons chili powder
2 teaspoons salt
1 teaspoon Dijon mustard

Cook the onions in the oil until tender.

Add rest of ingredients.

Bring to boil, stirring constantly.

NOTE: Use this to baste meat or poultry, or served over meat.

BUTTERS/DRESSINGS/ OILS/VINAIGRETTES

BUTTERS

CHILI-LIME BUTTER

½ pound butter, softened
1 tablespoon garlic, minced
Lime juice, from 1 lime
2 tablespoons cilantro, fresh, chopped
2 tablespoons chipotle pepper, minced in adobo sauce, plus…
1 teaspoon adobo sauce (or 1 teaspoon chipotle pepper, ground)
½ teaspoon cumin, ground
Salt
Pepper

At home:

Combine the butter, garlic, lime, cilantro, chipotle, and cumin.

Mix well.

Salt and pepper to taste.

Form into a log.

Wrap log in plastic wrap.

Store in an airtight container in the refrigerator, cooler, or freeze until ready to use.

GARLIC BUTTER

½ pound butter
4 garlic cloves, finely minced
Salt
Pepper

Put all ingredients into a food processor.

Mix.

Salt and pepper to taste.

Mix until smooth.

Remove.

Form into a log.

Wrap in plastic wrap.

Refrigerate for 2-3 days (or freeze for about a week).

GARLIC-CILANTRO BUTTER

To our recipe for **Garlic Butter** (See Above) add:

¼ cup of fresh cilantro, chopped
2 teaspoons lime juice, fresh

And…prepare as exactly as instructed for our Garlic Butter.

DRESSINGS

BLEU-CHEESE DRESSING

2 cups mayonnaise
2 cups buttermilk
2 garlic cloves, finely chopped
1 teaspoon garlic salt
8 ounces bleu cheese, crumbled
½ cup sour cream
Pepper, fresh ground, to taste.

Combine all ingredients.

Mix well.

Refrigerate.

OILS

CHILI OIL

1 cup of olive oil

NOTE: No need to use extra-virgin olive oil.

¼ cup red pepper flakes

Heat oil until it just starts to simmer.

Add the pepper flakes.

Remove from the heat.

Cool.

Store in a covered jar in the refrigerator.

NOTE: Shake well before using.

Will keep for 3-4 weeks.

GARLIC OIL

NOTE: We have a tendency to double, even triple, this recipe, because we use this on just about anything and everything, even as a replacement for the oil in pizza dough and salad dressings.

1 whole head of garlic
2 cups olive oil

Separate and peel the garlic cloves.

Bring the oil to a simmer.

Add the peeled garlic cloves and simmer for about 10-15 minutes on low, until garlic is golden brown.

NOTE: Be careful NOT to let the garlic get too dark or your oil will end up tasting bitter.

Let cool for at least 2 hours.

Refrigerate to infuse flavors.

Will last 2-3 weeks.

NOTE: We'll occasionally remove a garlic clove or two and mash them with a bit of oil as a more immediate spread for bread or Crostini.

GARLIC AND CHILI OIL

Garlic Oil (See Above)
1 tablespoon of red pepper flakes

Add pepper flakes to hot Garlic Oil.

Let stand for at least 2 hours.

Refrigerate.

Will last 2-3 weeks.

VINAIGRETTES

NOTE: For salads, we like to mix the vinaigrette in the bottom of the salad bowl, add the greens; then, toss.

VINAIGRETTE DRESSING #1

Combine 2 tablespoons of balsamic or red wine vinegar.

Slowly whisk in ¼ cup olive oil.

Add fresh herbs, such as 1 tablespoon finely minced basil, parsley, or rosemary.

NOTE: We find this one particularly good over sliced fresh tomatoes.

VINAIGRETTE DRESSING #2

Combine 2 tablespoons of balsamic or red wine vinegar.

Slowly whisk in ¼ cup olive oil.

Add ¼ teaspoon of pepper flakes, or 2 teaspoons chipotle puree.

VINAIGRETTE DRESSING #3

Combine 2 tablespoons of balsamic or red wine vinegar.

Slowly whisk in ¼ cup olive oil.

Add 1 minced garlic clove.

NOTE: This is another one we find particular good over sliced fresh tomatoes.

VINAIGRETTE DRESSING #4

Combine 3 tablespoons Champagne vinegar, ½ teaspoon Dijon mustard, ½ teaspoon Napastyle® gray salt, and ¼ teaspoon pepper.

Slowly whisk in ½ cup (plus 2 additional tablespoons) olive oil.

VINAIGRETTE DRESSING #5

½ cup salad oil
¼ cup sugar, or to taste
⅓ cup lemon juice, preferably fresh
½ teaspoon salt
Dash of pepper

Whisk the sugar, lemon juice, salt and pepper, together to dissolve the sugar in the bottom of the salad bowl.

Slowly whisk in the oil until thoroughly mixed.

NOTE: Dressing will be thick.

NOTE: Can be made up to a week ahead of time and refrigerated.

DESSERTS

For us, desserts, if and when we have them, usually consist of fresh fruit. Sometimes, while we're eating our main course, we just toss the fruit on our grill, which we've turned to low; the fruit usually ready to eat by end of the meal.

After a day in the sun, on the water, we're usually not in the mood for anything too sweet or heavy; although, we have included in BACK OF THE BOAT GOURMET COOKING a couple of the recipes we pull out for company and for special occasions.

Sometimes, too, while relaxing and watching a beautiful sunset, we simply enjoy either a glass of Knipprath Cellar's chocolate-flavored port-style "Au Chocolat!"…or Europa's delicious chocolate/wine combo, "ChocoVine"; the latter served over shaved ice, or in iced or hot coffee.

Banana Boat

Banana, small
Nutella®
Chopped nuts, your preference
Mini marshmallows
Whipped cream
Maraschino cherries, chopped

Place a small banana on its side on a piece of aluminum foil.

NOTE: Using a large banana often provides servings bigger than needed.

Carefully, slit the banana peel lengthwise.

Open the slit, and spread on the revealed banana a tablespoon of Nutella®.

NOTE: Don't get carried away with your stuffing, or the result can be really quite messy.

NOTE: We have used this recipe, by the way, substituting chocolate pieces, but it has never, in our opinion, worked nearly as well, as with Nutella®.

Sprinkle about a teaspoon of chopped nuts (your preference) along the Nutella®.

Add a small amount of mini marshmallows (not too many).

Seal the foil around the banana.

Put on a preheated grill, turned on low—for about 10 minutes.

Remove from the grill and carefully open the foil, being especially wary of venting steam.

Add whipped cream and diced cherries (if desired).

Serve.

Decadent Chocolate Dessert Pizza

½ pizza **Dough** recipe (see Pizza/Dough) omitting the garlic and herbs. Freeze the other ½ for some other time.
Xoçai® Power Squares®, coarsely chopped
Mini marshmallows
Banana, sliced
Nutella®
Maraschino cherries, chopped

Follow **Grilling Pizza** directions (See Pizza/Grilling Pizza) but grill only on one side.

Cooked side up, sprinkle with:

Xoçai® Power Squares®, as many as desired.

Add mini marshmallows.

Add banana slices.

Spoon on Nutella®

Put back on oiled grill until chocolate and marshmallows are melted. Crust should be lightly brown.

Sprinkle with chopped Maraschino cherries.

Recommended wine:

Townshend Cellars Huckleberry Port

FRUIT **C**RUMBLE

4 fruit of your choice: apples or peaches or nectarines or plums or....
Oil
1 stick of butter
½ cup brown sugar
1 teaspoon cinnamon
½ cup granola
Vanilla ice cream (See Desserts/...With Vanilla Ice Cream—below)

Preheat grill to medium.

Leaving skin on, cut in half, core, or pit the fruit.

Well oil the grate.

Brush fruit with oil.

Put fruit on grill, cut side down.

Grill fruit until lightly brown.

Remove fruit from grill and put in a bowl to cool slightly.

In a sauce pan, melt butter.

Cut cooled fruit into chunks.

Toss with half of the melted butter, ½ teaspoon cinnamon, and ¼ cup brown sugar.

In another bowl, toss the remaining butter, cinnamon, and brown sugar with the granola.

Divide the granola in 4 bowls.

Add the grilled fruit mixture to granola, dividing equally.

Top with scoop of vanilla ice cream, or Crème Anglaise.

Serves 4.

FRUIT CRUMBLE WITH VANILLA ICE CREAM

We purchased an Ice Cream Maker Ball. You can find them at Kitchen Shops, Target, or the Internet. They are fun to use. The ice cream is done in 20-30 minutes. You can also use it to make your favorite Crème Anglaise (follow recipe that usually comes with your Ice Cream Ball) to pour over Fruit Crumble.

NOTE: After putting ingredients in the Ball, your guests can have some fun and actually help, by kicking the Ball around. BUT no roughhousing, or you'll end up with a real mess on your boat!

STRAWBERRIES DIPPED IN XOCAI® CHOCOLATE FONDUE

20 Xoçai® Chocolate Nuggets®
2 tablespoons cream
¼ teaspoon instant espresso granules
2 tablespoons Chambord® liqueur
Strawberries, long-stemmed

Before you start dinner, put the Xoçai® Chocolate Nuggets®, cream and instant coffee granules in your fondue pot and set the pot in warm (not hot) water, and set total somewhere on your boat that's very warm but NOT in direct sunlight.

NOTE: Xoçai® chocolate doesn't have any waxes or fillers, so it melts nicely in low heat, and the instant coffee granules will dissolve.

When you're ready to serve, stir the Xoçai® chocolate, cream and coffee granules mixture until it's smooth.

Stir in the Chambord®.

Keep the mixture warm.

Use long-stemmed strawberries for dipping.

Serves 4 to 6.

RECOMMENDED WINE:

Latah Creek Muscat Cannelli.

WINE SORBET

This is a refreshing and ice-slushy way to serve wine on a hot day. You can use either white or red, and it doesn't have to be sweet wine, either.

Ice Cream Maker Ball
6 ounces water
½ cup sugar
10 ounces of your favorite wine

At Home:

Dissolve the sugar in the water over low heat.

Add the wine.

Cool.

On Boat:

Freeze according to the direction for the Ice Cream Maker Ball.

DRINK

WILLIAM—

Every boater has his favorite drink or drinks to bring along and enjoy while at sail—whether it be bottled water, soft drinks, even ice-cold beer. Bonnie and I enjoy wine. So, since I'm simultaneously writing my WILLIAM MALTESE'S WINE TASTER'S GUIDE: SPOKANE-PULLMAN WASHINGTON WINE REGION, as part of my WILLIAM MALTESE WINE TASTER'S DIARY wine series of books for Wildside/Borgo, and since Bonnie and her husband, Bruce, have been goodness-graciously ferrying me around to those various local wineries for tastings, you will have noticed that we've gone ahead and recommended several of these eastern-Washington wines, during the course of this book, that we've personally thought worked well with certain recipes. And, on occasion, we've mentioned other wines, both American and foreign, that we remember as having gone particularly well with a specific meal. Whether or not the reader finds these wines equally appealing, as complements for the very same food, considering just how subjective anyone's preference for wine can be, our recommendations are merely that—recommendations—and shouldn't be taken as THE GOSPEL ACCORDING TO BONNIE AND WILLIAM.

In this end-of-book DRINK section, we've merely provided the simple recipe for a recreational any-time drink Bonnie and I have mutually come to refer to as a "Xomosa"; we've found it energy-boosting, and a nice way to dilute champagne on hot days when there's a tendency to quench one's thirst by taking big gulps; okay, it can, also, make a less-than-stellar champagne taste better and not go to waste.

<u>Xomosa</u>

Champagne (good but not the best), chilled
Xocai® Xe® (the energy drink) chilled

Pour equal amounts of champagne and Xocai® Xe® into a glass.

Imbibe!

URLs

ABACELA VINEYARD AND WINERY
http://www.abacela.com

ARBOR CREST WINE CELLARS
http://www.arborcrest.com

BARILI CELLARS
http://www.barilicellars.com

BARRISTER WINERY
http://www.barristerwinery.com

BASALT CELLARS
http://www.basaltcellars.com

CHAIRELLO VINEYARDS
http://www.chiarellovineyards.com

GOATS DO ROAM
http://www.goatsdoroam.com

GRANDE RONDE CELLARS
http://www.granderondecellars.com

KNIPPRATH CELLARS
http://www.knipprathcellars.com

LATAH CREEK WINE CELLARS
http://www.latahcreek.com

LIBERTY LAKE CELLARS
http://www.libertylakewinecellars.com

LONE CANARY WINERY
http://www.lonecanary.com

MERRY CELLARS
http://www.merrycellars.com

MOUNTAIN DOME WINERY
http://www.mountaindome.com

NAPASTYLE®
http://www.napastyle.com/home.jsp

NODLAND CELLARS
http://www.nodlandcellars.com

OVERBLUFF CELLARS
http://www.overbluffcellars.com

ROBERT KARL CELLARS
http://www.robertkarl.com

SANTA EMA WINERY
http://www.santaema.cl

TERRANOVA CELLARS
http://www.terranovacellars.com

TOWNSHEND CELLAR
http://www.townshendcellar.com

TREZZI FARM FOOD & WINE
http://www.trezzibarn.com

VEUVE CLICQUOT PONSARDIN CHAMPAGNE
http://www.veuve-clicquot.com/

VINTAGE HILL CELLARS
http://www.vintagehillcellars.com

WAWAWAI CANYON WINERY
http://www.wawawaicanyon.com

WHITESTONE WINERY
http://www.whitestonewinery.com

RECIPE INDEX

NOTE: Main sections are shown in all-caps and boldfaced type, and subsections are shown just in boldfaced type.

Artichokes, 44
Asparagus, 45
Banana Boat, 164
Barbecue Sauce, 150
Basil Pesto, 134
Beef Steak, 86-87
Bleu-Cheese Buffalo Burgers, 80
Bleu Cheese Dressing, 155
Bonnie's Exotic Pasta Salad, 52
BREAD, 111-122
Breakfast Dogs, 91
Brian's Hot Wings, 98
Bruschetta, 112-118
Bruschetta with Apricot Jam or Orange Marmalade, 112
Bruschetta with Classic Tomato Basil Topping, 112
Bruschetta with Grilled Fresh Asparagus and Cheese, 114
Bruschetta with Non-Classic Bruschetta Topping, 116
Bruschetta for Breakfast, 117
Buns, 119-120
Buns from Long-Loaf Bread, 119
Buns from Round-Loaf Bread, 119

Burgers, 78-85
Butters, 152-154
BUTTERS/DRESSINGS/OILS/VINAIGRETTES, 151-161
Catch of the Day, 65
Caviar & Sour Cream, Potatoes with, 35
Cheese Spread, Dill Cream, 137
Cheese Spread, Herbed Goat, 139
CHICKEN, 97-104
Chili-Lime Butter, 42, 152
Chili Oil, 156-157
Chipotle Mayonnaise, 141
Chips, Potatoes for, 36
Chocolate Dessert Pizza, 166
Chocolate Fondue, 170
Cilantro-Garlic Butter, 153
Clams with Linguine, 106
Classic Basil Pesto, 134
Corn with Chili-Lime Butter, 42
Country Ribs, 93
Crab Cakes or "Burgers," 75
Crostini, 121-122
Crumble, Fruit, 168
Crumble, Fruit, with Vanilla Ice Cream, 169
Cucumber and Dill Sauce, 136
Decadent Chocolate Dessert Pizza, 166
DESSERTS, 163-172
Dill and Cucumber Sauce, 136
Dill Cream Cheese Spread, 137
DIPS/SALSAS/SAUCES/SPREADS, 133-150
Dough, Pizza, 124-127

Dressings, 155
DRINK, 173-175
Eggplant, Onions, Zucchini, and Other Squash, 46
EGGS, 39-40
Fiesta Tequila Lime Chicken, 101
FISH AND SEAFOOD, 63-76
Fondue, Chocolate, 170
Fruit Crumble, 168
Fruit Crumble with Vanilla Ice Cream, 169
Garlic and Chili Oil, 157
Garlic Butter, 153
Garlic-Cilantro Butter, 153
Garlic Oil, 156
Glazed Ham, 88
Glazed Ham with Pineapple, 89
Green Beans, 47
Green Eggs, 40
Grilling Pizza, 127-128
Guacamole, 138
Ham, 88-90
Herb-Grilled Shrimp, 67
Herb Pasta, 109
Herbed Goat Cheese Spread, 139
Horseradish Mayonnaise, 141
Hot Dogs, 91-92
Hot Wings, 98
Ice Cream, Fruit Crumble with, 169
Inside-Out Bleu-Cheese Buffalo Burgers, 80
Inside-Out Burgers, 78
Inside-Out Swiss Mushroom Burgers, 82
Inside-Out Taco Burgers, 83

Jalapeño Poppers, 30
Lemon Chicken, 103
Lime Chicken, Tequila, 101
Linguine, Clams with, 106
Marinated Grilled Lemon Chicken, 103
Mayonnaise, 141-142
MEAT, 77-95
Mushroom Burgers, 82
Mushrooms, 48
Mustard Sauce, 143
Nachos, 32
Oils, 156-158
Onions, 46
Oysters, 69
Other Vegetables from A-Z, 44-50
PASTA, 105-110
Pasta Salad, 52
Penne with Tomato, Mozzarella and Basil, 54
Peppers (Green, Yellow, Red), 47
Pesto, Classic Basil, 134
Pico de Gallo, 144
PIZZA, 123-131
Pizza **Dough, 124-127**
Pizza **Dough** with All-Purpose White Flour, 125
Pizza **Dough** with Whole-Wheat Flour, 125
Pizza Toppings, 128-131
Potato Salad French Style, 56
Potatoes, 34-38
Potatoes for Chips, 36
Potatoes for Stuffed Skins, 37
Potatoes with Caviar & Sour Cream, 35

POULTRY (CHICKEN), 97-104
Quick-and-Easy Salsa, 146
Rib-Eye, 86
Ribs, 93-95
SALADS, 51-62
Salmon, 71-76
Salmon on Cedar Plank, 71
Salmon/Shrimp/Crab Cakes or "Burgers," 75
Salmon Spread, Smoked, 148
Salmon Steaks with Spice Rub, 72
Salsas, 146
Sauces, 136
Scallions/Green Onions, 49
SEAFOOD, 63-76
Shrimp Cakes or "Burgers," 75
Shrimp, Herb-Grilled, 67
Shrimp Salad, 59
Shrimp Salad with Penne, 62
Smoked Salmon Spread, 148
SNACKS, 29-38
Sorbet, Wine, 172
Sour Cream, Potatoes with, 35
Spicy Barbecue Sauce, 150
Spinach Salad, 58
Spreads, 137-140, 148
Squash, 46
STARTERS AND SNACKS, 29-38
Steak, Beef, 86-87
Strawberries dipped in Xocai® Chocolate Fondue, 170
Strawberry Spinach Salad, 58
Stuffed Skins, Potatoes for, 37

Swiss Mushroom Burgers, 82
Taco Burgers, 83
Tequila Lime Chicken, 101
Tomatoes, 50
Unbelievable Shrimp Salad, 59
Unbelievable Shrimp Salad with Penne, 62
VEGETABLES, 41-50
Vinaigrette Dressing #1, 159
Vinaigrette Dressing #2, 159
Vinaigrette Dressing #3, 160
Vinaigrette Dressing #4, 160
Vinaigrette Dressing #5, 160
Vinaigrettes, 159-161
Wasabi Mayonnaise, 142
Wine Sorbet, 172
Xoçai® Chocolate Fondue, 170
Xomosa, 175
Zucchini, 46

ABOUT THE AUTHORS

BONNIE CLARK and husband Bruce were born, raised, met, and married in the Spokane, Washington, area, and have since raised their family there. Bonnie's interest in cooking started at a very early age when her Mother went to work, and Bonnie started planning and preparing dinners for the family. Her passion for cooking and entertaining grew, bolstered by her close connection and participation in her mother-in-law's professional catering business. Finally, enough family and friends told her that she "should write a cookbook" that she decided that, maybe, it was time she did just that. As it happens, her cousin, help-/cookbook author, William Maltese, fellow gourmand, wine connoisseur, and avid boater, was looking to do the same thing, and BACK OF THE BOAT GOURMET COOKING was born.

http://www.facebook.com/bonnieclark

Bonnie's Xoçai® chocolate-for-sale site:
http://www.richesinchocolate.com

WILLIAM MALTESE, the author (along with Adrienne Z. Milligan) of the best-selling THE GLUTEN-FREE WAY: MY WAY for the Borgo Press Imprint of Wildside Press, was born in the Pacific Northwest, has a B.A. in Marketing/Advertising, and spent an honorable tour of duty in the U.S. Army where he achieved the rank of E-5. He started his career writing for men's pulp magazines, and has since had published more than 200 books, fiction and nonfiction, in every genre, while being honored with a listing in the prestigious *Who's Who in America*. For more information on William, check out his websites:

http://www.williammaltese.com
http://www.facebook.com/williammaltese
http://www.facebook.com/flickerwarriors
http://www.facebook.com/draqual
http://www.myspace.com/williammaltese
http://www.myspace.com/draqual
http://www.myspace.com/flickerwarriors
http://www.myspace.com/maltesecandlegallery
http://www.theglutenfreewaymyway.com
William's Xoçai® chocolate-for-sale site:
http://www.mxi.myvoffice.com/williammaltese

www.ingramcontent.com/pod-product-compliance
Lightning Source LLC
LaVergne TN
LVHW041620070426
835507LV00008B/353